"*Intercession.* When I first heard the word, many years back, it conjured otherworldly images: wild-eyed prophets calling down fire, stern-visaged lawgivers cleaving seas, cave-dwelling saints raising the dead. Tricia Rhodes' *Intimate Intercession* shows otherwise: that even ordinary folk like you and me are called to stand in the gap. What's more, she persuades that intercession is the best path to intimacy with and imitation of Jesus, and that as we walk that path, Jesus more and more invites us to be eyewitnesses to and holy vessels of his redemptive presence in the earth. This is a great book on prayer for the simple reason that it actually makes you want to pray."

—Mark Buchanan, Author of *The Rest of God*
and *Your God Is Too Safe*

"With passion, warmth, and humble transparency, Tricia McCary Rhodes makes intercession accessible to every believer. Whether you've been praying for years, or have only just started, whether you feel good about your progress or think you have a long way to go, whether you're praying with joy and anticipation, or are weary from the battle, *Intimate Intercession* will free you to relax in the mystery and enjoy the intimacy that comes in relating to God through prayer."

—Cynthia Bezek, Editor of *Pray!*

"Although I've traveled the worldwide prayer movement for over twenty years, Tricia's latest gift to the church makes me want to learn how to pray all over again! The writing style is fresh and compelling. The reflections offer both breadth and depth. The insights are profoundly life-changing yet easily applied. But above all, it is Tricia's passion for the exaltation of God's Son, woven into this book in a hundred ways, that stirs me to desire greater intimacy with Christ in His sovereign work in the lives of others. Which is precisely what prayer is all about in the first place!"

—David Bryant
Founder, PROCLAIM HOPE!
Author, *Christ Is All! A Joyful Manifesto*
on the Supremacy of God's Son

INTIMATE
INTERCESSION

THE SACRED JOY
of PRAYING FOR OTHERS

TRICIA McCARY
RHODES

W PUBLISHING GROUP
A Division of Thomas Nelson Publishers
Since 1798

www.wpublishinggroup.com

Published by W Publishing Group, a Division of Thomas Nelson, Inc., P.O. Box 141000, Nashville, Tennessee 37214.

W Publishing Group books may be purchased in bulk for educational, business, fundraising, or sales promotional use. For information, please e-mail SpecialMarkets@ThomasNelson.com.

All Scripture quotations, unless otherwise indicated, are from the New American Standard Bible (NASB), © 1960, 1977, 1995 by the Lockman Foundation.

Scripture quotations noted THE MESSAGE are from *The Message.* Copyright © 1993, 1994, 1995, 1996, 2000, 2001, 2002. Used by permission of NavPress Publishing Group.

Scripture quotations noted NLT are from the *Holy Bible*, New Living Translation, copyright © 1996. Used by permission of Tyndale House Publishers, Inc., Wheaton, Illinois 60189. All rights reserved.

Library of Congress Cataloging-in-Publication Data

Rhodes, Tricia McCary.
    Intimate intercession : the sacred joy of praying for others / Tricia McCary Rhodes.
      p. cm.
Includes bibliographical references.
ISBN 0-8499-0563-X
    1. Intercessory prayer—Christianity. I. Title.
BV227.R46 2005
248.3'2—dc22

2005020421

Printed in the United States of America

05 06 07 08 QW 7 6 5 4 3 2 1

This book is dedicated to seven intercessors who are dear to my heart: Carol and Susie—my beloved sisters who have prayed from the start, and Angie, Barb, Linda, Lois, and Vicky—my faithful Monday morning sister-warriors.

CONTENTS

CONTENTS

Finding the Right Fit

The year I turned five I took to trying on my mother's shoes. I remember one pair in particular—shiny black patent leather, toes like the beak of a duck-billed platypus and four-inch heels, stilettos that could do some serious damage. When I stepped into them, I'd slide down until my entire feet were stuffed like putty into the toes. Then I'd shuffle across the linoleum, swaying my hips as I glanced at the armoire mirror to admire my style. Those shoes hurt like the dickens, and I never went very far in them—just back and forth, ankles twisting this way and that.

Every now and then, though, I'd catch a glimpse of someone besides my scrawny self in that mirror, someone sophisticated, bigger than life. Those were whispers of whimsy, dreams and dares of what I might someday be. But before long, tiring of the viselike grip on my feet, I'd don my scuffed saddle shoes and run off to race my brother in the field behind our house or play hopscotch on our sloping driveway. This I understood: While pretending to be someone I was not had its moments of magic and mystery, the stuff of ordinary life was a lot more fun.

Something about the spiritual disciplines always makes me want to try on someone else's shoes, as if mine are just too commonplace. Take, for example, intercession. Even the word itself sounds exotic—it conjures up visions of sophisticated saints with bigger-than-life qualities. And why wouldn't it? I think of Rees Howells, the miner who may very well have changed the course of World War II through his prayers. There's Praying Hyde, who spent untold nights weeping over souls in India until revival broke out in the nineteenth century, and David Brainerd, whose diary of prayer for Native Americans has impacted intercessors for centuries now. Legend has it that he would kneel outside the villages of those he longed to reach and become so lost in prayer that he could sink two feet into the snow without even realizing it.

I'm star-struck by intercessors of my generation as well. One woman I know prays separately for every single nation on earth—all 192 of them—at least once a month. There are those who faithfully lift up government leaders in the United States and beyond, and others who walk city streets daily, interceding for the needs there. Last week I received an e-mail urging me to join not one, but three different prayer ventures—21 days, 91 days, and a 40-day fast for consecration before national elections.

When I get wind of these things or read another book or hear the latest prayer story, before I know it I'm sliding down, being squeezed into some narrow place like putty. Trying to walk a mile in someone else's shoes, I wobble along with dogged determination to endure the discomfort so I can be a *real* intercessor. I may even glance in the mirror to admire my style, hoping to see something besides my very ordinary self.

Why am I telling you this? For one thing, I want you to know from the start what kind of person I am. I'm not an expert on intercession, though I'm prone to dress up like one every now and then. Since God called me to write this book, I have compared myself endlessly to those I consider *real* intercessors, and always, I come up short. This is no false humility—it is the honest truth. I have a few good stories, but a lot more fits and failures over a lifetime of seeking to embrace the incredible ministry of intercession. Another reason I mention this is that I suspect you may struggle as I do. Perhaps you've even picked up this book with a mixture of misgiving and hope at the same time. That's exactly how I feel writing it.

Here's the thing: There's nothing wrong with setting our sights on being like those who really know how to pray, those who've learned to love the inner room so much that power seems to emanate from their very pores. These are the saints who can give us vision and hope—moments of whispered whimsy and dare-to dreams of what can be. But if intercession is ever going to come naturally and be as fun as I think God intends it to be, there's only one pair of shoes that will work for either of us. Like my saddle shoes of yore, our shoes may be scuffed and well worn, but they belong to us and can get us where we need to go every single day of our lives.

Try to remain true to the simplicity of your unique calling in Christ.

As you meander through the pages of this book, I pray you'll begin to see for yourself that your shoes fit you best in the places God wants to take you in prayer. If, while reading, you stumble onto some new path or discover an interesting insight about intercession that you'd like to try on for size, go ahead—but try to remain true to the simplicity of your unique calling in Christ. God doesn't take any pleasure in any of us trying to be someone we're not. Rest in His grace and enjoy yourself—there's not much else to it.

Oh, and by the way, if you catch me sashaying around and admiring my style—bear with me—I'll get over it soon enough.

CHAPTER ONE

IN SEARCH OF A DEFINITION

The Beauty and Simplicity
of Intercessory Prayer

I think about people I know, the saints
with their swollen ankles or their knobby
hands, the rickety prayer warriors who
don't have the physical strength to open
a pickle jar but who set whole legions of
demons flying for cover whenever they
kneel. Some are pious misfits, holy
eccentrics. Most are just ordinary, with
nothing but the presence of God to dis-
tinguish them from all the other people
on the face of the earth.

MARK BUCHANAN[1]

Intercession is a spiritual discipline fraught with paradox. It can be as mysterious as a shooting star one minute and as mundane as breathing in and out the next. Sometimes it feels like a dance with destiny, but more often like a labor of love. Personally, I've had some great adventures in intercession, and even an occasional walk on the wild side, yet there are days I'm put off by the monotony of it. Intercession is an art form, a craft with delicate nuances developed over the course of a lifetime, yet even a child can do it. (Perhaps that is why we tend to come at it with a sort of nonchalance when we ought to be standing gape-jawed at the possibilities before us.)

I've read some books on intercession and pondered numerous definitions and still I'm not sure what to say here, but let me begin with this. I once heard of a Christian leader who didn't believe in praying for his own needs. Whenever he asked for anything from God, it was for someone else's benefit. His reasoning was that he could count on God's taking care of him, since He always had, and besides, praying for other people was just more enjoyable. Although I'm not sure I agree with his theology on prayer (Jesus *did* tell us to ask for our daily bread), I do believe this man is an intercessor, because the cornerstone of intercession is the act of pleading someone else's case before God in prayer.

From bedtime prayers to huddles in hospital waiting rooms, from e-mail prayer chains to collective cries for revival, from forty-day fasts to Sunday benedictions—intercession can be at the heart of each of these. Even the Wednesday night prayer meetings I was weaned on, the kind that usually turned into a litany of personal or family ailments (Aunt Gracie's hiatal hernia, Bob's lost job, Diane's depression, and of course the *unspoken requests*), in all likelihood included intercession.

It just seems to me that we often elevate this form of prayer to a lofty plane on which most of us never feel at home. Isn't there some simple way to approach intercession? Some definition that draws us in, no matter what level of maturity we're at or what degree of knowledge we've acquired?

The Bible sheds an interesting light on the question. The word *intercession* itself rarely appears, and there are few texts that could even be considered direct teaching on it (we'll get to those later). What Scripture offers instead is a cornucopia of simple stories that show people praying for one another in all kinds of situations.

There are the Sunday school favorites—Abraham pleading for Sodom to be spared and Aaron and Hur holding up

Moses's arms as he interceded over the battle below. But consider some of these lesser-known prayers from the Old Testament: The servant Eliezer prayed that God would bring the perfect bride for Isaac, and Isaac prayed for his own wife in her barrenness. In his dying hours, Jacob prayed a blessing over each of his twelve sons, and Boaz prayed that Ruth would experience a full reward for her labor as well as the comfort of God's sheltering wings. Elijah prayed for healing for King Jeroboam's withered hand, Job prayed for his friends (the pious ones who had judged him during his time of distress), and David pleaded with God not to take his own sin out on the Israelites.[2]

The New Testament also unveils an assorted array of specific requests people made on behalf of others. Jesus asked His Father to keep Peter strong in faith when He knew he was going to be sifted by Satan. He prayed for a unity among believers that would be so powerful the world would stand back in awe. He wept over Lazarus and then spoke His prayer out loud so that those who were watching would grow in their understanding of God. In His dying moments Jesus prayed for forgiveness for His enemies, and His final good-bye before ascending to heaven was a prayer of blessing that filled the hearts of those left behind with joy.[3]

Paul prayed for healing for the father of Publius on the island of Melita and pleaded for the salvation of his Hebrew kinsmen. He prayed that the Roman church would have unity of mind and for those in Ephesus to have spiritual eyes to see and know the mysteries of God. He asked that the

Colossian believers would come to know God's will fully and that the Thessalonians might be counted worthy of their calling.[4]

In the same way, Paul was always appealing to others to pray for him. He encouraged his fellow saints to ask that he'd be delivered from evil men and that other believers would accept his ministry. He told Philemon to pray he'd be released from prison and asked the Roman church to entreat God to send him their way soon. Because he so longed to be used to spread the gospel, Paul often urged the churches to pray that his efforts would be successful.[5]

In other New Testament examples, we find Stephen appealing on behalf of those who were stoning him, that they not be held accountable for their horrific acts, and Peter and John praying for the Samaritans to receive the Holy Spirit. The fledgling church prayed for Peter upon his arrest, and Epaphras labored fervently for the Colossian believers that they would stand mature and complete in God's will.[6]

Clearly the act of one person pleading on behalf of another is a common theme throughout Scripture. But are all of these actually examples of *intercession*? Does intercession differ from petition or supplication, or simply making another's needs known to God? If so, how? I believe the answer can be found by looking at Moses, the humble intercessor of the Old Testament. Moses engaged in many conversations with God on behalf of the Hebrew people that he led out of Egypt. On more than one occasion, he pleaded for God to have mercy when the people had been extremely rebellious. Psalm 106 tells of the critical role Moses played at one point when God was furious with them: "He said that He would destroy them, had not Moses His chosen one stood in the breach before Him, to turn away His wrath from destroying them" (v. 23). Moses "stood in the breach." This is an awesome concept and seems to symbolize the very heart of what makes intercession unique.

When Scripture speaks of a gap or a breach, it refers to something that is no longer as it ought to be, something that has been torn apart or broken down, leaving things in a state of disrepair. In this case, God had made a covenant with Israel—He would be their God, and they would enjoy a relationship of unprecedented favor as His beloved. But within days after He'd miraculously delivered them from Egypt, they began to act as if they'd never known Him or experienced His goodness. They griped and complained and finally created a god of their own liking in the form of a golden calf.

The covenant relationship between God and His people was now broken down, their rebellion having created a breach that seemed irreparable. In His great anger, God let Moses in on His plans to destroy the obstinate bunch and start over, using him to make a great nation from scratch. Moses rejected God's offer, though he had plenty of reasons to be mad at the Israelites himself. Instead, he took their side, aligning himself with the very ones who had given him such grief as a leader. Standing in the gap between them and God, Moses pleaded for Him to have mercy on them one more time.

As I look back on the last few days, I have talked with

> This, I believe, is intercession—to *stand in the gap* between God and needy people.

God concerning a variety of situations—a friend who was struggling with outbursts of anger and my son's first day back at school after summer break. I've prayed for a young neighbor who is disillusioned with God and for missionary friends experiencing an unprecedented heat wave. I've made requests for the leaders in our church and for a prodigal niece and her grieving parents. In some cases I simply shared the person's needs with God, as I saw them. But in other cases when I prayed, my spirit experienced a unity—an identifying with the person and the deficiency they faced as if it were my own.

When I prayed for my niece, I felt a sense of personal outrage at what the enemy has stolen from her. As I lifted up our church leaders, I was overcome with a longing for joy and power as I sensed that one of them felt trapped in a dry and barren land. When I prayed for my friend, I experienced deep desire for her freedom and mine from the fleshly struggles that stem from living in a fallen world.

This, I believe, is intercession—to *stand in the gap* between God and needy people, our hearts bonded to theirs as we plead their cases in prayer, regardless of what they have done or haven't done to deserve His intervention. We see this most extravagantly displayed in our Lord, who walked the earth as a friend of sinners, identifying with us in all aspects of our humanity. In a prophetic word, Isaiah wrote of the Christ: "He poured out Himself to death, and was numbered with the transgressors; yet He Himself bore the sin of many, and interceded for the transgressors" (53:12).

To a world in disrepair, Jesus came. He stretched out His arms on Calvary's tree and spanned the great breach between holy God and sinful man by allowing Himself to be numbered with cheaters and prostitutes and boasters and gossips and drunkards and gamblers and gluttons and sinners of every sort. He entered into your point of need and mine, interceding for us even to the point of death, so that the floodgates of God's mercy could flow once again through His shed blood.

Here's the most amazing thing: Jesus has invited you and me to join Him in bridging the gap between a dark and desperate world and His Father, who waits on high to be gracious to the people that inhabit it. Scripture tells us that even now Jesus ever lives to make intercession for us (Hebrews 7:25). We are never more like Christ than when we connect with another in their pain or their sin and choose to carry their burdens in prayer, asking God to bring His kindness to bear on the disrepair in their lives.

Intercession is simple, yet profound. It is a precious privilege granted to each one of us. Through it we are brought into the very heart of the One who reigns above all and holds the worlds together by His power. From that place we live out our incredible destiny as co-laborers

> We are never more like Christ than when we connect with another in their pain or their sin and choose to carry their burdens in prayer.

with Christ. I believe if we could see it, if we could just catch a glimpse of the wonder in each whisper of intercession, we'd be hooked for life.

WHAT, ME, AN INTERCESSOR?

One night many years ago, I awoke from a deep sleep with a distinct sense that someone had spoken. The word I heard was *intercessor*. I lay there a few minutes, wondering what it meant and where it had come from, and then I heard it again. *Intercessor.* It wasn't an audible voice, but it seemed as real as if my husband had sat up in bed and said it himself. I knew that this was more than some random thought. Wide awake by now, I climbed out of bed and went to the living room to wait. Feeling a bit like the boy Samuel, I told God He could speak anytime—that His servant was listening. Nothing happened.

Although it was four in the morning, I decided to stay up and pray. Over the course of the next several weeks, I woke up at the same ghastly time every day, but I didn't feel tired or resistant, and in fact was excited about getting up and meeting with the Lord (trust me, this was a miracle). I never heard the word *intercessor* again, but I was certain God was calling me to an exciting new way of life. I couldn't wait for Him to make me a full-fledged intercessor.

But then one morning, and the next and the next, I woke up not to the dark of night, but to the sun streaming through my bedroom window. I tried setting my alarm for a few days to recapture the early-morning vigils but had to drag myself out of bed, that joyful sense of eagerness a thing of the past. I soon settled back into my old quiet-time schedule, but the memory of that voice, of that word—*intercessor*—haunted me like a tune I couldn't get out of my mind.

I began to read everything I could find on the subject of intercession, soaking up information from books and articles and Scripture passages like a sponge, but the more I read, the worse I felt. Don't get me wrong—the stories were exciting and the instruction was rich—but all I could think of was how far I was from what I was supposed to be. How would I ever live up to such noble aspirations?

Why would God call me to a discipline I seemed unable to achieve? Could I be an intercessor if I would just bite the bullet and force myself to spend hours on my face every day? Did all real intercessors carry burdens with such sobriety that they would gladly go without food or drink or sleep in their desire to see God intervene? Was I just (pick one) lazy, resistant, lackadaisical, rebellious, ignorant, hardhearted, or immature? Did I suffer from some spiritual stronghold or personality defect? This was a frustrating time, for no matter what I did or how hard I tried, I could never get away from the feeling that I hadn't yet become a *real* intercessor.

And then one day a couple of years later, God spoke about it again and His answer stunned me—it still does. In my spirit I sensed Him saying this: *Tricia, when I whispered the word* intercessor *to you years ago, it was not because there was something I wanted you to become, but rather because it was something you already were. I just wanted you to know.*

> If you are a Christian, you are, by your very nature, an intercessor.

Me? An intercessor? How could this be? Immediately the objections started buzzing around inside my head. But I pondered what I'd heard, turning the words over and over in prayer until a sense of peace descended, and I knew something had changed. For the next several months, I put away the books and messages and articles and tried to listen to what God was saying to me. How can I explain this? At some point I just stopped trying to be something I wasn't and began to walk in the wonder of what God said I already was. Today I know this for certain—I am an intercessor—I have it on the highest authority. Just to write those words fills me with joy.

I want you to know this and believe it as well. If you are a Christian, you are, by your very nature, an intercessor. When God saved you, He filled you with the life of Christ, who is always interceding. And though our propensity to identify with another's pain or cry out on their behalf out of love and compassion may be buried beneath a load of guilt and a pound of flesh, intercession is every believer's call and destiny, joy and crown.

Please hear me—there are no chosen few. Intercession is not a spiritual gift bestowed on select saints. This myth of a special call has of late created an entire cottage industry of books and conferences and causes. Pastors during the past decade have been inundated with counsel and even condemnation from those who consider themselves uniquely set apart from the rest of the body to be *intercessors*.

So I will say it one more time: If you are a Christian, you are an intercessor. I am not writing this book to tell you what you ought to be, but to help you discover what you already are so that you can experience the wonder of it. What burns brightly within you is a heart to intercede, and it has been there a long time. (Repeat after me: *I am an intercessor.*)

The Universal Qualifier

People who read books on prayer are usually hoping to learn how to pray more effectively. If that describes you, you'll be eager for me to give you some handles on how to get started or move beyond the point you are at right now. Should you commit an hour a day to pray for others? Should you fast consistently or spend one night a week in prayer? Do you need to have some weekly plan that ensures every need is prayed for regularly?

The answer to all these things, for now, is no. What I'm going to ask you to do instead is to set aside your expectations of what this journey is supposed to be like. Let go of all the "should's" and "ought to's" that come at you when you think of prayer. Resist the nagging voices that tell you if you would just work harder or learn more or become more spiritual, you'd finally get this whole intercession thing right.

Andrew Murray wrote that "the sense of impotence is the soul of intercession."[7] Don't rush

"The sense of impotence is the soul of intercession."

past this blessed truth. Do you feel powerless at times in intercession or even impotent to begin or persevere in prayer? Do you feel inadequate? Do you look at yourself and wonder what God is thinking when He calls you an intercessor? Do you watch others farther along the path and question whether you'll ever get there?

If your answer is yes to any one of these questions, then there is incredibly good news for you. The very thing that makes you doubt yourself is that which actually qualifies you to be an intercessor. Why? Because God is opposed to the proud, but gives grace to the humble (James 4:6). The very foundation of humility is the ability to see our own need and impotence, our helplessness to do the things we want to do. This is the soul of intercession because it opens the door for us to receive God's grace, and "grace is God's transforming power to do in us what we cannot do for ourselves."[8]

WHAT IS YOUR STYLE?

One of the most important steps in embracing the ministry of intercession is to find out what feels natural as far as the way in which we pray. This is a process similar to one every new writer goes through to discover their "voice" as they begin to practice putting words to paper. When I first started to write, the things I had to say sounded a lot like whatever book I happened to be reading at the time. The following sage advice from a classic primer on writing by William Zinsser speaks volumes and set me on a course of freedom as an author:

You will reach for gaudy similes and tinseled adjectives, as if "style" were something you could buy in a style store at the mall and drape onto your words in bright decorator colors. There is no style store. Style is organic to the person doing the writing, as much a part of him as his hair, or if he is bald, his lack of it.[9]

This is a great truth for writers and intercessors as well and brings us back to my confession at the start of this book. Though I am always tempted to try on someone else's shoes or to emulate the "style" of those I consider *real* intercessors, I have learned, and I hope you will, too, that there really is no style store. In writing *and* in prayer, style is organic to the person doing it—which means you and me. How we intercede, when we intercede, the words we use, the tone we adopt, how long we intercede—all of these are things that come from the core of who we already are in Christ.

In one tongue-in-cheek article, Alice Smith draws our attention to the different styles on display when intercessors come together. She tells of the Mercy-Motivated Intercessor praying with "passion and tears, a fever erupting in his heart," until the Administrative Intercessor gets irritated and wishes she could organize the meeting and give it some direction. There is the Warfare Intercessor, who goes into spiritual battle as she "waves her hands and fiercely rebukes the rulers of darkness," while those around her wish someone would give her a sedative! The Prayer-List Intercessor seems too "calculated and routine" to some,

Each of us has unique gifts, personalities, and preferences, and recognizing this is critical to our enjoyment in intercession.

and the Seasoned Veteran intimidates everyone into silence with his or her perfect prayers. Finally, the Off-Track Intercessor breaks in with prayer for his neighbor's lost puppy.[10] A bit exaggerated, perhaps, but close enough to reality that we all can relate to it.

Each of us has unique gifts, personalities, and preferences, and recognizing this is critical to our enjoyment in intercession. So what is your style? How can you tell if you're being yourself in prayer or trying to be someone else? Zinsser likens taking on someone else's style to a bald man's putting on a toupee. He may look young and handsome at first, but people always do a double take, because something just isn't quite right. It's the same with intercession. When you find yourself slipping into someone else's style, things just won't feel quite right to you or those who might be joining you in prayer. There is something comfortable about our own style, an ease that can come only through practice.

As we move forward in this book, my desire is that you will grow in the simple grace of intercession, avoiding pretentiousness like the plague. Though you may experience a nagging pressure to live up to the stories and lives and prayers of others, I hope you will resist the temptation. There is no style store; there's just you and me, learning how to pray—one prayer at a time—until we operate with the flair of natural-born intercessors.

Practicing Prayer

At the end of each chapter, we will pause to meditate on the prayers of other saints—some monologue and some dialogue with God. There are a few reasons I think this will be meaningful. First, we will see how varied intercessory prayer can be and catch a glimpse of God's heart through praying people. Second, this rich heritage can expand our vision as it reveals how we are one small link in a great prayer chain that stretches across the course of history and spans the globe today. This can build our faith in powerful ways.

Here's a format you can follow, but feel free to establish your own:

- Read these prayers silently through once, pondering the heart and meaning in them.
- Read each one aloud, as if it were your own.
- Journal your thoughts about what you have read, then write your own prayer.
- Read your written prayer to the Lord aloud.

A Prayer of Daniel for God's People
(Daniel 9:4–19 nlt)

O Lord, you are a great and awesome God! You always fulfill your promises of unfailing love to those who love you and keep your commands. But we have sinned and done wrong. We have rebelled against you and scorned your commands and regulations. We have refused to listen to your servants the prophets, who spoke your messages to our kings and princes and ancestors and to all the people of the land.

Lord, you are in the right; but our faces are covered with shame, just as you see us now. This is true of us all, including the people of Judah and Jerusalem and all Israel, scattered near and far, wherever you have driven us because of our disloyalty to you. O Lord, we and our kings, princes, and ancestors are covered with shame because we have sinned against you. But the Lord our God is merciful and forgiving, even though we have rebelled against him. We have not obeyed the Lord our God, for we have not followed the laws he gave us through his servants the prophets. All Israel has disobeyed your law and turned away, refusing to listen to your voice.

So now the solemn curses and judgments written in the law of Moses, the servant of God, have been poured out against us because of our sin. You have done exactly what you warned you would do against us and our rulers. Never in all history has there been a disaster like the one that happened in Jerusalem. Every curse written against us in the law of Moses has come true. All the troubles he predicted have taken place. But we have refused to seek mercy from the LORD our God by turning from our sins and recognizing his truth. The LORD has brought against us the disaster he prepared, for we did not obey him, and the LORD our God is just in everything he does.

O Lord our God, you brought lasting honor to your name by rescuing your people from Egypt in a great display of power. But we have sinned and are full of wickedness. In view of all your faithful mercies, Lord, please turn your furious anger away from your city of Jerusalem, your holy mountain. All the neighboring nations mock Jerusalem and your people because of our sins and the sins of our ancestors.

O our God, hear your servant's prayer! Listen as I plead. For your own sake, Lord, smile again on your desolate sanctuary.

O my God, listen to me and hear my request. Open your eyes and see our wretchedness. See how your city lies in ruins—for everyone knows that it is yours. We do not ask because we deserve help, but because you are so merciful.

O Lord, hear. O Lord, forgive. O Lord, listen and act! For your own sake, O my God, do not delay, for your people and your city bear your name.

A Prayer of Anselm of Canterbury for His Enemies

Anselm was a philosopher and Benedictine monk who went on to become the archbishop of Canterbury in the eleventh century. His writings on the existence of God were both scholarly and prescient, bringing understanding to searching souls even to this day.

Almighty and tender Lord Jesus Christ,
Just as I have asked you to love my friends
So I ask the same for my enemies.
You alone, Lord, are mighty.
You alone are merciful.
Whatever you make me desire for my enemies,
Give it to them.
And give the same back to me.
If I ever ask for them anything
Which is outside your perfect rule of love,
Whether through weakness, ignorance or malice,
Good Lord, do not give it to them
And do not give it back to me.
You who are the true light, lighten their darkness.
You who are the whole truth, correct their errors.
You who are the incarnate word, give life to their souls.
Tender Lord Jesus.
Let me not be a stumbling block to them
Nor a rock of offense.

My sin is sufficient to me, without harming others.
I, a slave to sin,
Beg your mercy on my fellow slaves.
Let them be reconciled with you,
And through you reconciled to me.[11]

LOOKING AHEAD

What is God really up to with intercession? Why does He call us to it? If we could see what He sees when we intercede, what would we think? How would it impact our desire to pray? These are some of the things we're going to look at next, as we step back and examine the big picture from God's perspective. I like to call it the *Great Invitation*, and I hope you'll come along.

CHAPTER TWO

THE GREAT INVITATION

*Our Holy Calling as
Apprentices in the Creator's
School of Prayer*

*But is He not the King of glory? All He
is and all He does is glory . . . and this is
the God who bids us come to Him in
prayer. This God is our God and He has
gifts for men.*

ANONYMOUS[1]

Several years ago I set out to find a way to pray more intentionally for the nations of the earth. Annual mission trips to remote villages in northeast India and Bangladesh had stirred my heart in a fresh way, and Jesus's claim that His house was to be one of prayer for *all* nations weighed on me with healthy conviction—not the guilt-laden stuff, but the joy of true yearning. Though I prayed for missionaries I knew and for the group of unreached people my church had adopted, I found myself experiencing a growing desire to learn how to intercede for places and people I'd never heard of—to expand my horizons, you might say.

One April morning I decided to make the plunge. But how should I begin? *Operation World*, Patrick Johnstone's amazing work, lay before me—the one with all the facts, plus a prayer strategy for every known people group. I'd used it often for reference and was always fascinated with its snapshots of the world and its wonder—sights and sounds and smells beyond my reach. But when I had tried to work through it page by page in prayer, my mind just couldn't seem to absorb all that information, and I would lose interest within a few days.[2]

So I sat there that morning considering my options, when out of the corner of my eye I saw the globe on the shelf across the room. Walking over to it, I nonchalantly gave it a spin, closed my eyes, and put out my finger. (I feel the need to pause here and say that I had never done this before and haven't done it since, but this is a true story and it makes a great point, so bear with me.) When I opened my eyes and looked down the length of my finger, I saw a small country, wedged between Iran and Pakistan, called Afghanistan.

Feeling pretty silly, I decided I'd try the whole thing over again, expecting a completely different continent this time. Imagine my surprise when I discovered my finger resting in exactly the same place. Now I was beginning to wonder, and I decided this might be a good time to talk to the Lord about it. With Gideon-like boldness, I told Him I'd be happy to intercede for the little country I knew nothing about, but if He had anything to do with it, would He please make my finger land there one more time. I closed my eyes, spun the globe harder than before, and waved my hand around in the air before letting my finger land. When I looked, it was on—you guessed it—Afghanistan.

I can't say I felt like much of an intercessor by the time I got around to praying that morning,

I could only shake my head as I pondered the possibility that God really had been in on my globe-spinning escapade.

but I offered a few requests for Afghanistan anyway—for those who'd never heard the gospel and for the believers who might be facing persecution there. After that, the experience sort of faded away with the busyness of daily life. A few days later, however, a news clip on the radio caught my attention. It told of a group of men in custody for plotting terrorist attacks. Though they were arrested in Israel, the interrogation revealed that they had just left a training camp in Afghanistan.

Today the whole world is well acquainted with those infamous Al-Qaeda camps, but this was months before September 11 and the first I'd ever heard of them. Were it not for my time of praying over Afghanistan, I doubt I even would have given it a second thought. When the news ended that day, I could only shake my head as I pondered the possibility that God really had been in on my globe-spinning escapade.

As it turned out, those few seemingly random moments catapulted me into one of the greatest intercession adventures I've ever known. It had all the elements of a good drama—intriguing characters, mystery, suspense, and some surprise twists that culminated in a glorious climax. I still stand back in awe at the experience and chuckle a little every time I think of how it all began, with me acting like some kind of game-show contestant as I set out to pray for the nations. More about that later.

THE GOD WHO DARES

Let me first ask a question that might already be on your mind: Was God actually directing me into intercession for

What is God thinking when He calls mortals like you and me to the ministry of intercession?

Afghanistan, or was the whole thing some kind of fluke? At the time I really didn't know, but looking back, I have no doubt that He was behind it all. To me, the greater question is, Why? What is God thinking when He calls mortals like you and me to the ministry of intercession? Why does He always seem to be throwing down dares for us to pray, like some gauntlet at our feet? Ponder the following—and remember that this is the God of the universe speaking to us:

- Then you will call upon Me and come and pray to Me, and I will listen to you. (Jeremiah 29:12)

- Call to Me and I will answer you, and I will tell you great and mighty things, which you do not know. (Jeremiah 33:3)

- Ask of Me, and I will surely give the nations as Your inheritance, and the very ends of the earth as Your possession. (Psalm 2:8)

- So I say to you, ask, and it will be given to you. (Luke 11:9)

- If you ask Me anything in My name, I will do it. (John 14:14)

- Ask and you will receive, so that your joy may be made full. (John 16:24)

When I see all these Scriptures clustered together like this, I feel a bit slow, as if God must have been keenly aware that I'd have a hard time getting the point. The truth is, our Maker wants us to ask, because He loves for us to get in on what He is doing in the world, and to that end inspires our hearts with desires that He can fulfill, for His glory and our joy.

Perhaps I can illustrate it this way. Recently I attended a museum exhibit called "Saint Peter and the Vatican," which traced the history of the Catholic headquarters in Rome by using its invaluable works of art and historical artifacts. Saint Peter's Basilica, which tradition states was built over the tomb of Peter the Apostle, is an awesome structure that houses some of the most famous paintings and sculptures in the world.

Constructed in the sixteenth century under the commission of Pope Julius II, this was to be a far more magnificent edifice than the original building, which had lain in a state of disrepair for years. Though the new design involved almost all the well-known architects of the day, the most famous was Michelangelo, who created the plans for its extraordinary dome ceiling.

The exhibit I attended included a series of drawings done a hundred years later depicting the various stages the dome had gone through during construction. One of the drawings showed half of the dome cut away, revealing the intricate detail on the inside. In the picture, the dome towered beneath a sky full of clouds, one of which carried Jesus and Peter. The two seemed to be in deep conversation—Jesus pointing to

Can you see yourself there, seated with Christ in the heavenlies, poised to participate with Him in transforming hearts and lives and families and cities and nations?

the dome and Peter nodding—suggesting that they were guiding the building process together.

That image stirred something in me. I can just imagine being the one up there with Christ on the cloud, looking out over the world as He points out some need—a family in distress or a soul in despair or a church in disarray—and shares His heart to rebuild with me. I begin to see what can happen through His eyes. Soon, bursting with desire, I urge Him to go forward with His plans. With a hearty smile, He begins the project while I reverently watch the miracle of which I have somehow become a part.

Can you envision this? Can you see yourself there, seated with Christ in the heavenlies, poised to participate with Him in transforming hearts and lives and families and cities and nations? This is the great invitation God extends to you and me through the ministry of intercession. It can happen every day in dozens of ways—the possibilities are endless. An awareness of this will bring a sense of purpose to even our most mundane tasks.

This week as I volunteered in the front office at my son's high school—answering phones, directing visitors, and assisting students—a mom called to have her son released. She shared how he'd suffered from serious depression that week, and she didn't know why. He'd called her in tears at lunch, saying he couldn't stay at school one more minute. I hung up the phone with a heavy heart. When the young man came to pick up his pass, the look of despair in his eyes pierced me, and I couldn't help but pray for him over the course of the afternoon.

I don't know the outcome of that story, and I may not until eternity. But do you see the beauty of this? An ordinary afternoon as a school volunteer suddenly turned into something of significance. Not only did Jesus share His heart with me through the pain I felt over the situation, but He also enabled me to become a channel of His mercy to my world through one phone call and a few short prayers.

We are meant for so much more than we often realize.

Here's the point: We are meant for so much more than we often realize. It's difficult to believe that an act as simple as a breath of prayer can have some kind of cosmic import, a place in the grand scheme of things. But it is true, for intercession springs first and foremost from the heart of God, whose brilliant vision for the future pulses even now from the throne room of heaven. He is ever inviting you and me to join Him on this amazing adventure, to live life—day in and day out—on the edge of holy expectancy.

Understanding Our Destiny

Imagine with me, for a moment, existence before time and space and matter. God simply *is* and there is nothing else.

Worshiping the creature instead of the Creator, humanity is trapped in an endless pattern of joyless self-destruction (Romans 1:25).

Everything about Him shines with beauty and perfection. Within His being resides the fullness of Deity—all power, goodness, mercy, justice, righteousness, joy, peace, love, and an infinite number of other attributes. Complete in Himself, the Almighty has need of nothing. He is one God beaming forth as three—Father, Son, and Spirit—who dwell as a community within an atmosphere of mutual delight.

Some theologians suggest that joy within the Godhead bubbled up and over, until one day—like a volcano that couldn't be contained—the Lord exploded with creative energy. First, He formed a universe in which He could put His glory—the essence of His character, attributes, and ways—on display. Then came the crown of creation—men and women who, because they were made in His own image, would be able to experience an intimate union with Him, enjoying the glorious mystery hitherto known only by the three-in-one God. In this unfolding plan, the cycle of divine delight could continuously expand—generation after generation of glory-bearers filling the earth until the globe radiated with God's beauty like a ball on fire.

If you or I could travel today outside this life and world and planets and galaxies and every created thing, I believe we would find beyond the pale this exquisite tale of Trinitarian joy, one glimpse of which would flood our hearts with unspeakable yearning. Why? Because we would know instinctively that we were made to be a part of this—that nothing else we've ever experienced could possibly compare. It would seem, perhaps, that we had come home at last.

But the world we live in is a dry and weary land where human beings are haunted by hunger for something outside their reach. Souls once branded with the image of Christ now bear an earthly one. A people destined for glory hide in the shadows of sin, ever turning to lesser gods—whether idols of wood and stone or those of the heart—as they seek futilely to satisfy the desires of their souls. Worshiping the creature instead of the Creator, humanity is trapped in an endless pattern of joyless self-destruction (Romans 1:25).

The imprint of God's image on our being, hopelessly marred in the Fall, is what Jesus came to seek and to save. When He redeems us for Himself by His blood, a miracle of rebirth takes place, enabling us to reclaim that which we were always meant to possess—the capacity to revel in and reflect the glory of God. Drawing us into the holy circle of triune joy, God calls us to fulfill our destiny as glory-bearers whose beams will one day cover the face of the earth (Numbers 14:21; Habakkuk 2:14).

GOD'S GLORY, OUR JOY

I know these are lofty thoughts, but please press in with me here. If we don't get the connection between God's glory and our joy, we'll never see intercession as the mystery and wonder God intends it to be, nor will we experience the freedom and power available to us in prayer. The measure of our desire and fruitfulness in intercession or any other spiritual discipline depends on the degree to which we grasp that our greatest joy is found in living for God's glory.

But what does this mean? When I was growing up, preachers talked a lot about God's glory, usually to keep wayward parishioners in line. In my teenage years, "Do everything for the glory of God" was like a mantra, chanted like a liturgy to keep us from going to dances or smoking cigarettes or lying to our parents if we did. When I was a high-school girl sitting at home on a Friday night, you could never have convinced me God's glory had anything to do with a pursuit of joy or a life of destiny.

I'm not sure those preachers really understood what the glory of God was. I know I didn't. This is not surprising, for Scripture itself can seem confusing on the subject. At times the Bible refers to God's glory as all that He is—His wondrous beauty revealed to us, as in "The heavens are telling of the glory of God" (Psalm 19:1). But at other times, the Bible speaks of our giving God glory or glorifying Him. For example: "O God, we give glory to you all day long and constantly praise your name" (Psalm 44:8 NLT). These may sound like two different things, but they are actually flip sides of the same coin—you can't have one without the other.

Let me try to explain. For us to give God glory, we must first know and experience and enjoy His glory—the wonder of His beauty—for ourselves. Think about this. Could you rave about the nuances of chocolate—bittersweet, semisweet, white, milk, European Cadbury, or American Hershey—if you hadn't tasted the various possibilities? Would you go to great lengths to obtain a piece if you'd never had the experience of one of those sweet, creamy morsels melting in your mouth? Or consider the ocean. Would you fear its power if you'd never heard the roar of its waters at high tide? Could it stir you with awe if you'd never been near enough to walk its sandy beach, to feel the pulsing of waves like a drumbeat beneath your feet? In the same way, can you give God the glory due Him in your heart and words and actions and life if you aren't tasting His goodness or savoring His sufficiency or living in His love or, in other words, gaining His glory?

These two things—gaining God's glory and giving Him glory—come together beautifully in the ministry of intercession. For example, yesterday I joined in a prayer time for a woman in her sixties who was desperate for freedom from some things that had kept her in bondage for decades. As we interceded on her behalf, we saw God's tender compassion and felt His abundant grace. We marveled at His wisdom and were in awe at His power. Each of us in that room experienced the glory of God as He set one captive free. Deeply grateful, we ended our time together praising His name, giving God glory out of the overflow of joy in our hearts.

For us to give God glory, we must first know and experience and enjoy His glory—the wonder of His beauty—for ourselves.

I think this is how Solomon felt at the dedication of the temple. In the midst of the celebration, God's glory so filled the place that the priests couldn't even continue to minister. Solomon then burst into a spontaneous prayer of blessing for all God had done and began to intercede for his own people and for others who might visit the temple in years to come. Listen to the cry of his heart:

> When foreigners hear of you and come from distant lands to worship your great name—for they will hear of you and of your mighty miracles and your power—and when they pray toward this Temple, then hear from heaven where you live, and grant what they ask of you. Then all the people of the earth will come to know and fear you.
> (1 Kings 8:41–43 NLT)

When we experience God personally, we cannot help but yearn to see Him made known and so, like Solomon, we intercede. We stand on behalf of others and cry out for some manifestation of God's glory—His power or love or compassion or justice or righteousness or kindness or holiness—knowing that when He answers, people will respond in worship and honor and praise and changed lives. And as we intercede, we come full circle by once again experiencing the wonder of God's glory in the fellowship we are sharing with Him. This is what makes intercession a mystical delight that can draw us to our knees again and again.

CHECKING OUR MOTIVES

What do you think is the first thing that comes to mind when people hear the word *intercession*? Joy? Adventure? Living on the edge of expectancy? Now, let's get personal. Does the idea of intercession translate into a pursuit of joy for you? For example, do you anticipate church prayer meetings with pleasure? When you hear of

> Wouldn't it be wonderful if joy were the fuel that energized us to intercede?

someone in need of prayer, do you view it as an exciting opportunity? Do you see standing in the gap for others as a privilege, a way in which you can fulfill your destiny?

The last thing I want to do here is cause more guilt about prayer—we've got enough of that to go around already. But on the other hand, wouldn't it be wonderful if joy were the fuel that energized us to intercede? If we could rid ourselves of lesser motives that in the end don't work anyway? I believe Satan's greatest strategy is to rob us of our joy by distorting the truth so that we continue serving God, but with all the wrong motives. Here are a few beliefs that have wreaked havoc with my own intercession journey through the years.

Believing My Prayer Life Limits God

The ministry of intercession, if we're not careful, can tend to make us feel like little sovereigns, as if our prayers or lack of them limits God in some way. Thoughts like these, subtle or blatant, are a burden that may temporarily prod us to intercede, but in the end they break down because we just can't live with the guilt that goes along with our weaknesses.

Scripture makes it clear that only God is sovereign, and

thus nothing we do or fail to do can sabotage His work in this world. God holds absolute power over heaven and earth. No one can thwart His plans, for He is always doing exactly what He wants to do. Nothing is impossible to Him. Basically, this means God holds *all* the cards.[3]

If you are like me, you may be asking whether it makes any difference if we pray or not. And the answer is yes, it does—Scripture affirms this. There is a dynamic correlation between our prayers and the movement of God on the earth, which we will explore in a later chapter. What I want to do for now is to strip us of this motive that springs from fear that God's work won't get done, first because it is unbiblical, and second because, frankly, it will never sustain us in prayer. God's Word on the subject is indisputable—nothing we do or fail to do as intercessors can ultimately thwart His plans, for as He says, "Everything I plan will come to pass, for I do whatever I wish" (Isaiah 46:10 NLT).

Believing God Needs Us to Get the Job Done

Closely related to the notion that our lack of prayer limits God is the idea that He needs us to get the job done. I struggled with this for years, having heard all my life that the fate of men's souls, at home and in heathen lands, rested on my shoulders, as if God needed me for the task of securing their salvation. This is preposterous. God is God, and if He were deficient or lacking in any way, then He would cease to be God. Consider Paul's exhortation to the scholars and philosophers in Athens:

The God who made the world and all things in it, since He is Lord of heaven and earth, does not dwell in temples made with hands; nor is He served by human hands, as though He needed anything, since He Himself gives to all people life and breath and all things. (Acts 17:24–25)

God does not need us. Though there are mystery and wonder in the reality that He has chosen to cooperate with men and women to do His work on this earth, the truth, as Paul went on to profess, is that it is in Christ we live and move and have our very existence. What could we possibly offer that the Father doesn't have at His fingertips in the person of Jesus Christ, His Son, and the power of His Holy Spirit?

I want to try to drive this point home because I have a feeling that this notion of God needing us creeps up in subtle ways we may not recognize. Let me take a little liberty and rephrase some thoughts Paul presented to the Corinthian believers by way of a few questions: Are you wise about the things of the Spirit? Do you have a reputation for power in prayer? Do you possess a wealth of knowledge from reading books and going to conferences, or because you come from a long line of praying believers (1 Corinthians 1:25–31)?

If so, then just in case you're ever tempted to boast, be prepared for God to put a person in your path whom you wouldn't even think of as intercessor material. Stand back and watch as the Holy Spirit comes in power through the prayers of this simpleminded saint who can't show up at church on time and doesn't know the least thing about spiritual mapping or forty-day fasts! (Foolish things to confound the wise, don't you see?)

I have to say that I'm first in line when it comes to struggling with this kind of spiritual pride. I'm learning, though, that while thinking God depends on me—my knowledge, my zeal, my commitment—might feel good at times (mostly when I'm at the top of my game), when the pressure builds I want to run the other way. Who but Jesus can carry the weight of the world? I know I cannot.

So in those times when we fail to pray (and we often will), let's rest in the knowledge that God is going to get the job done. We may miss the blessing of it, but God doesn't need us—He has a whole host of intercessors waiting in the wings when we're not available. This can be the most freeing truth we'll ever learn and, contrary to what we might think, in the end will empower us to intercede more than ever before.

Believing It Is Up to Us

How do you feel when you hear about all-night prayer meetings or lengthy fasts or well-established intercession plans? What goes on inside when you read of someone who devotes large blocks of time to prayer or who never misses a quiet time? Do you shake your head and wonder why you can't get with the program? Do you feel guilty and withdraw a little more or determine to try a little harder? If so, you may be operating under the subtle assumption that the ability to embrace the ministry of intercession is up to you.

If you were to talk to veteran warriors who have walked in paths of prayer for a long time, they would be the first to affirm that any success they've experienced has nothing to do with them. The truth is that though intercession can feel at times like labor, it is from start to finish the grace of God working in us and never the result of our own abilities or efforts (1 Corinthians 15:10).

Jesus is Alpha and Omega in our intercessions; He is at work from beginning to end. He knocks at our heart's door with someone's need, and then gives us a desire to open that door. He speaks words of guidance about what to pray and then enables us to hear His voice. He calls us to pray and imparts the grace to join Him in our prayers. Then, when we do offer up our requests, it is His power that secures the answer. We honestly bring nothing to the table except a willing heart and a listening ear, and even when those aren't readily available, He promises to work in us for His good pleasure until they are (Philippians 2:13). Everything is from Him and through Him and to Him, and when we live under this banner of truth, He will always receive the glory (Romans 11:36).

It may take some time to rid ourselves of misguided motives that place us at the center of the intercession paradigm. But until we understand that *it is all about Him*, we'll never walk in the freedom of knowing that *it is all up to Him*. Our call is to learn to live in the wonder of who God is, humbled that in spite of our flaws and failures and frailties, He continues to invite us to partner with Him in the joy of seeing His glory manifested throughout the world.

AND NOW . . . THE REST OF THE STORY

When God opened my eyes and heart to the small country of Afghanistan that spring morning in 2001, I had no idea what would come of it. I began to study about the country the day I heard of the terrorist training camps there, trying to understand what it was God wanted me to pray for and why He'd called me to this subject in particular.

So, when I picked up my newspaper on August 7 and read of a group of international and Afghan aid workers that had been arrested for proselytizing, my heart stirred with anticipation. I followed every detail of the story over the next few days, searching Web sites from the Middle East and Europe for any tidbit of information I could find. I soon discovered that among the twenty-four who'd been taken into custody were two young American women—Heather Mercer and Dayna Curry. Some of the most serious charges were against them because they'd shared the *Jesus* video and other Christian materials with a Muslim family—something forbidden by strict Islamic law.

As time went on, I began to see that the girls' captivity was one piece of a much larger story. I read the country's tumultuous history, including efforts by various groups to overthrow the oppressive Taliban government. I discovered that many other believers worked in Afghanistan—social workers, doctors, nurses, and teachers—all with the goal of sharing Christ's love as God opened doors for them in this country so shut off from the gospel message.

On some days there was no news about the girls, and on

others I got snippets of information that indicated their lives were in grave danger. With each word I gleaned, I would intercede for Heather and Dayna, feeling as if they could be my own daughters. At one point some of their family members and a pastor traveled to Afghanistan to try to secure their release, but they were put off after being informed that the penalty for proselytizing could be death. It was an agonizing time. My heart became so burdened at one point that I felt compelled to share the things I was hearing. With an e-mail to a few friends, a prayer chain began that soon grew to more than a hundred names. Every time there was any news, I sent it out so that we could all pray wisely. (I found out later that scores of similar prayer chains had sprung up all over the world.)

Then came the events that would change the fabric of American life and send shock waves around the world. For the second time in history, the United States was attacked on its homeland when terrorists—trained in Afghanistan—flew airplanes into buildings, taking the lives of almost three thousand people. Like all Americans, I was sobered and saddened by these events.

But something else captivated my heart as I watched the Twin Towers burn that day, and that was the little country that had spawned such a colossal affair, and the jail cell in its capital where two young American believers were imprisoned. I feared for their safety even more in light of these developments. For a short time it seemed the Afghan government would try to use them as bargaining chips in the face of possible U.S. retaliation, but by September 20, when

President Bush demanded their immediate release, the Taliban had severed all contact.

The rest, I guess you could say, is history—the strikes on Afghanistan as the United States joined with rebel and coalition forces to overthrow the Taliban and search for the terrorist mastermind, Osama bin Laden. Every single day I looked for some word, for the smallest piece of news about the aid workers, my burden for their well-being becoming almost an obsession. Though there was rarely anything to share, I continued to send out e-mails reminding others to intercede.

As I continued to pray for those girls, concern for others who suffered under such oppressive rule in that country rose up within me. Compassion for the persecuted church there and desire for religious freedom began to permeate my prayers. One night in a small gathering at my church, it seemed as if the Holy Spirit poured out a passion for that country upon everyone in attendance. Energy filled the room as people wept and pleaded with God to intervene for the sake of His name and the afflictions of the Afghan people.

The U.S. air strikes on Afghanistan began October 7, and by early November the rebel forces had gained the upper hand. When they swept into Kabul, the people welcomed them with open arms as the Taliban fled to the city of Ghazni, taking the aid workers with them. We got our first news in a long while as reports detailed what the girls had left behind—some laundry, some food, and a piece of paper on the window sill that appeared to be a list of songs they might have used for worship the night before. When I heard this, I wept.

They say you can tell how important certain events are in your life by the details you remember from when you got the news. If that is true, then the rescue of Heather Mercer and Dayna Curry was monumental for me. I remember every aspect of the moment—where I was, what I was wearing, the time of day, etc.—when I heard that the girls had set fire to their scarves in a field outside Ghazni, thus revealing their location to the U.S. Special Forces, who picked them up. I watched Heather's and Dayna's Pakistan news conference on TV and was overcome as I saw for the first time the faces of these women for whom I'd interceded over the past three months. I could only rejoice at their

What if we believed that praying for others is akin to embarking on the greatest adventure of all?

strength as they praised God for His faithfulness and spoke of their desire to go back to Afghanistan to finish the work they'd begun.

I share this lengthy tale for one reason—to demonstrate the joy of intercession when God chooses to draw us in for His purposes. Whether those girls were rescued or whether they had lost their lives as millions of martyrs who have gone before, God is always about the business of shining forth the beauty and worth of His name. And if we choose to join Him—through the little prayers we offer up day in and day out, and on those rare occasions when our souls take flight on the wings of intercession—the journey will be one of ineffable joy.

WHAT IF . . .

What if we really believed that intercession is more about fulfilling our destiny than completing some kind of Christian obligation? What if we believed that praying for others is akin to embarking on the greatest adventure of all, rather than living up to some nebulous spiritual standard? What if, instead of racking up successes or cataloging our failures, we lived in a state of awe that the Lord of the universe has invited us to join Him in the dance of life? Maybe we would decide at last to pick up the gauntlet God continually throws down before us and accept His dare—to just ask for His glory and our joy.

PRACTICING PRAYER

Once again we will pause to meditate on the prayers of other saints. Here's a format you can follow, but feel free to establish your own:

- Read these prayers silently through once, pondering the heart and meaning in them.
- Read each one aloud, as if it were your own.
- Journal your thoughts about what you have read, then write your own prayer.
- Read your written prayer to the Lord aloud.

A PRAYER OF ABRAHAM FOR THE PEOPLE OF SODOM

(ADAPTED FROM GENESIS 18:23–32 NLT)

ABRAHAM: Will you destroy both innocent and guilty alike? Suppose you find fifty innocent people there within the city—will you still destroy it, and not spare it for their sakes? Surely you wouldn't do such a thing, destroying the innocent with the guilty. Why, you would be treating the innocent and the guilty exactly the same! Surely you wouldn't do that! Should not the Judge of all the earth do what is right?

GOD: If I find fifty innocent people in Sodom, I will spare the entire city for their sake.

ABRAHAM: Since I have begun, let me go on and speak further to my Lord, even though I am but dust and ashes. Suppose there are only forty-five? Will you destroy the city for lack of five?

GOD: I will not destroy it if I find forty-five.

ABRAHAM: Suppose there are only forty?

GOD: I will not destroy it if there are forty.

ABRAHAM: Please don't be angry, my Lord. Let me speak— suppose only thirty are found?

GOD: I will not destroy it if there are thirty.

ABRAHAM: Since I have dared to speak to the Lord, let me continue—suppose there are only twenty?

GOD: Then I will not destroy it for the sake of the twenty.

ABRAHAM: Lord, please do not get angry; I will speak but once more! Suppose only ten are found there?

GOD: Then, for the sake of the ten, I will not destroy it.

A Prayer of Saint Patrick of Ireland (AD 433)

Patrick was a missionary to Ireland whom God used to convert almost the entire nation from paganism to Christianity. Though the excerpts below sound more like an affirmation of faith, these sentiments can be powerful as a tool to begin a time of intercession.

I arise today
Through a mighty strength, the invocation of the
    Trinity,
Through a belief in the Threeness,
Through confession of the Oneness
Of the Creator of creation.

I arise today
Through God's strength to pilot me;
God's might to uphold me,
God's wisdom to guide me,
God's eye to look before me,

God's ear to hear me,
God's word to speak for me,
God's hand to guard me,
God's way to lie before me,
God's shield to protect me,
God's hosts to save me
From snares of the devil,
From temptations of vices,
From every one who desires me ill,
Afar and anear,
Alone or in a multitude.

I summon today all these powers between me and evil,
Against every cruel merciless power that opposes
    my body and soul,
Against incantations of false prophets,
Against black laws of pagandom,
Against false laws of heretics,
Against craft of idolatry,
Against spells of women and smiths and wizards,
Against every knowledge that corrupts man's body
    and soul.
Christ shield me today
Against poison, against burning,
Against drowning, against wounding,
So that reward may come to me in abundance.

Christ with me, Christ before me, Christ behind me,
Christ in me, Christ beneath me, Christ above me,

Christ on my right, Christ on my left,
Christ when I lie down, Christ when I sit down,
Christ in the heart of every man who thinks of me,
Christ in the mouth of every man who speaks of me,
Christ in the eye that sees me,
Christ in the ear that hears me.

LOOKING AHEAD

One thing has the power to keep us from experiencing inter-cession as this glorious adventure, and that is our lack of passion for God's glory. But how do we get more passion? The wondrous reality is that God wants to give us this far more than we could ever want to gain it. To that end, Jesus seeks every day to draw us into an intimate knowledge of Him. (I don't mean the accumulation of facts and ideas but the biblical idea as in Adam *knew* Eve.) When we learn how to sit at His feet, our love for His character, His ways, His attributes, and everything about Him will grow by leaps and bounds. Could anything be more disarming than this?

❧

CHAPTER THREE

THE CONTEMPLATIVE INTERCESSOR

*Beholding the Face of Christ
as We Lift Others Up*

*To pray is to grasp heaven in one's arms,
to embrace the Deity within one's soul,
and to feel one's body made a temple of
the Holy Spirit.*

CHARLES HADDON SPURGEON[1]

Have you ever had a secret dream, an aspiration to do something completely beyond your own capability? Perhaps we all do. For example, I've always wanted to be an artist. I am entirely envious of sculptors and painters and various sorts of craftsmen who can express the creative urges the rest of us have, but don't know what to do with. Every now and then I bravely pull out a sketchbook and a pencil, only to be disappointed as it soon becomes apparent that my skills have not improved. I guess I keep hoping that somewhere deep inside me there is an artist who will one day find her way out.

Today I have the privilege of writing in a friend's loft apartment where a large print of Rembrandt's *The Return of the Prodigal Son* hangs on the wall. I'm enamored with the way the light plays on that picture—the golden glow around the son on his knees and the mother hidden in the shadows, almost invisible. Disdain coupled with weariness emanates from the face of the older brother, who stands off to the side. The look in the father's nearly blind eyes as he bends down to embrace his son tells a gripping tale of profound affection. This is truly a masterpiece.

And I'm struck with the thought—what if I had been born in the seventeenth century to Rembrandt Harmenszoon van Rijn? And what if from my earliest years he had allowed me to stand at his side in the studio where he crafted such works? Would he have spoken with me of color and shadow and space and lines and the ways in which these things interact on canvas as he stood before his easel each day? Would he have taught me the principles of mixing pigments or shared his opinions on the downsides of various materials? Could it be that at some point he might have even offered me the brush and held his hand over mine so I could add a stroke to the brilliant rendering taking shape beneath his touch? Would I have become an artist just by virtue of having been Rembrandt's child?

These kinds of thoughts are a theme with me. During my vacation last summer, we camped beside the edge of a river that flows through the bottom of Kings Canyon in the Sequoia National Forest. Each morning, surrounded by redwoods and serenaded by the sound of water rippling across the rocks, I would watch the sun as it made its way up and over the top of those vast canyon walls. Without fail as I took in that scene from within the hollow of a massive broken tree trunk, the desire to capture the experience on canvas would rise up within me. I could almost feel the brush between my fingers.

And then one morning it came, a thought so simple I

don't know why I'd never considered it before: The desire I have to create—to form and fashion and craft and construct—exists because I am made in God's image. I am a child of the Master Designer. His creative energy is written on my DNA, so to speak. What does this have to do with intercession? Is it possible that our prayers for others and for our world might be one of the ways God provides for us to express the deepest creative urges of our souls? That His plan is to use these yearnings to draw us to Himself again and again, that we might know the joy of being used by Him to fulfill His purposes on this earth?

Think about what this would mean. Each day as God works on the masterpiece of a world He is filling with His glory, He calls you, His child, to come close—to stand right beside Him and learn, like an apprentice, but with every familial privilege. You are allowed to enter His studio whenever you want—to watch and listen as He explains what He is doing and why. Maybe He will tell of how these hues combine to form the perfect color for this church's lack of vibrancy, or why this texture is exactly what that young woman needs to bring out the graces that lie hidden beneath the whitewash over her heart.

Are you with me? Can you envision the day your Father the Artisan turns and asks you to blend some shades for His work at hand? You begin with

Is it possible that our prayers for others and for our world might be one of the ways God provides for us to express the deepest creative urges of our souls?

> *The most profound privilege of a prayerful life is not in getting answers to prayer— as amazing as that can be— but through the intimacy we experience with the Lord of the universe.*

the oil of His Spirit and then stir in a promise from His Word. Adding a sprinkle of faith and a dab of desire, you hold up your palette for Him to approve. Smiling with pleasure, God takes those colors you've put together and applies them to the canvas of a broken life or a demonized tribe or a hurricane-ravaged community.

The incredible reality is that we serve a God who not only answers prayer but also offers us the most tender intimacy as we partner together in one creative endeavor after another. This is why I have come to believe that it is the *process* of intercession that brings our greatest reward rather than the *product*. The most profound privilege of a prayerful life is not in getting answers to prayer—as amazing as that can be—but through the intimacy we experience with the Lord of the universe, who delights to share the secrets of His heart with us.

THE HEART OF INTERCESSION

I've titled this chapter "The Contemplative Intercessor" because it cuts to the core of what we need most in learning to stand in the gap in prayer. To be contemplative means to spend time in the quiet of God's presence, seeking His face and meditating on His Word as we grow in our knowledge of Him.[2] When contemplation and intercession work in tandem, they create a dynamic spiritual chemistry. From the wellspring of a life that communes with Christ in the quiet, the practice of lifting up the needs of others in prayer naturally flows forth. Why? Because when we sit at God's feet and learn from Him, we cannot help but see things as He sees them, and His heart pulses with holy desires for the people of this world.

Several years ago I watched as a longtime friend seemed to be wearing herself out in ministry to very needy people. One day I suggested that she might be more productive if she got involved with some folks who clearly wanted to grow in Christ. Although I was trying to be helpful, this advice wounded my friend, causing her to feel as if I had questioned her effectiveness and never really understood her heart and gifting.

We set aside a time when we could meet to try to find some common ground to restore our relationship. I wrestled with this for days, wondering what I could do, since I believed that the things I'd said were true and felt fairly certain that my motives had been right. The morning we were to meet, I spent some time in silent worship and meditation before God. The thought came to ask God to show me my friend as He saw her, which I did. Immediately the Holy Spirit flooded my mind with a picture of the woman who broke the alabaster bottle over Jesus's feet. Then I heard these words: *She gives extravagantly of herself without any thought of return. This is how I see her.*

Convicted instantly for my arrogance, I realized that

though I saw my friend as having a lack of balance, this simply was not the way God viewed her. As I pondered His words and pictured her face, I soon became overwhelmed with awe at the ways she displayed His love so generously to the least of these. This led to a precious time of intercession as I sought God's face and asked His blessing over her ministry and her life.

When we met a few hours later, I related all the things God had shown me. We cried and prayed together, feeling as if we were on holy ground, our relationship restored. Years later that experience still brings tears of gratitude to my eyes. I won't easily forget the taste of God's presence as He unveiled His heart to me that morning. The time I had spent in contemplation enabled me to see my merciful friend as He did, and this in itself was a great treasure. But beyond that, having experienced God's heart toward her has made praying for my friend a blessed privilege ever since.

Intercession that does not spring from this kind of intimacy with God will lack both power and joy. I remember speaking with a missionary once who told me she could not possibly spend her quiet times getting to know God because she would never get through the list of people she'd committed to pray for. As I probed, it seemed to me that she didn't find much joy in her daily times of prayer, but felt compelled to do them. She was hoping I could offer some means of becoming more effective at intercession and simply could not see that something greater was at stake. I believe God, by His grace, will still use her intercession, but like Martha, she is missing out on the one thing that is needful, the better part of communing with Christ (Luke 10:42).

Think back to the Rembrandt illustration. If I had been his child, he could have sent me to the finest school in the area to get the education I needed to become an accomplished artist. Though I might have produced some worthwhile pieces, imagine what I would have missed along the way— special memories of those moments with him and nuances about the craft that he alone could have taught me. And I never would have known that sense of having secretly partnered with him to create the masterpieces the world enjoys.

Do you see what I am saying? We can go to classes and read books and get the latest and greatest tips on how to intercede, but these types of instruction can never compare with the legacy of learning to pray by our Father's side. We can have our detailed plans and monthly focuses and community-wide gatherings, but these will not produce the joy of prayer where Christ's heart becomes ours by virtue of an intimate walk with Him, which is the greatest reward of contemplative intercession.

"I HAVE CALLED YOU FRIENDS"

In one of the most amazing statements He ever made, Jesus described to the disciples what He intended His relationship with His followers to look like:

> No longer do I call you slaves, for the slave does not know what his master is doing; but I have called you

friends, for all things that I have heard from My Father I have made known to you. (John 15:15)

Stop for a moment and think about this. Jesus calls you His friend, His familiar and favored companion. The word translated "friend" here is one we might use to describe the best man at a wedding, only with a much more significant role. In the Jewish culture, this person had to be someone so highly esteemed that he could be trusted not only to extend the marriage proposal, but also to complete all of the wedding details. Because marriages were always arranged, the friend often knew the bride and her family well before the groom ever set eyes upon her.

So what does this mean to us as intercessors? The incredible truth laid out here is that, because we are friends of Christ, He willingly entrusts us with the things that are most precious and important to Him. When we pray for another, it is as if He has esteemed us highly enough to let us have a part in putting together some of the details of His glorious future—the wedding of the Lamb and His bride, the church!

What does this look like on a practical basis? We can learn much from two of the men the Bible refers to as friends of God—John the Baptist and Moses. Both men demonstrated a deep humility concerning the unique status they were granted in their relationship with God. Let's begin with John. One day when some of his followers had expressed concern that he was losing popularity to the new Rabbi named Jesus, the wilderness prophet compared himself to a groom's best man, saying, "The friend of the bridegroom, who stands and hears him, rejoices greatly because of the bridegroom's voice. So this joy of mine has been made full" (John 3:29). From John's perspective, being a friend of the Bridegroom afforded him the privilege of standing close and listening to Christ's voice, something that produced abundant joy within him.

Has this been true for you? Do you delight to hear Jesus speak? Do you stand close by His side, waiting for a word of instruction or some aspect of His plan that you might have the privilege to fulfill through intercession? Do you read His Word, cherishing its nuances and rejoicing in its truths that can give breadth and depth to the things you pray on another's behalf? Do you take the time to sit in silence before God when you intercede, listening for the sound of His voice instead of storming the gates of heaven with yours?

This is no small matter. Hearing our Good Shepherd speak is the birthright of each of us who has been brought into the fold through His saving grace (John 10:27). It is the very thing Jesus sets forth as proof of His friendship with us.

I have called you friends, for all things that I have heard from My Father I have made known to you. Christ intends to make known to you and me that which is on the heart of His Father—this is what it means to be His friend. Can you think of a greater wonder?

Hearing our Good Shepherd speak is the birthright of each of us who has been brought into the fold through His saving grace (John 10:27).

Willingness to listen demonstrates the kind of humility we desperately need in prayer. King Solomon understood this, admonishing us, "Do not be hasty in word or impulsive in thought to bring up a matter in the presence of God. For God is in heaven and you are on the earth; therefore let your words be few" (Ecclesiastes 5:2). Because God is in heaven and we are on earth, He knows the end from the beginning, while we have only the tiniest slice of life to glean from and are ill prepared to pray from His perspective. Our flesh fights for its own way, the evil one sets out to confuse and discourage us, and we live in a world that places man at the center of every thought. To pray the mind of Christ for others requires that our own minds be renewed in His presence on a daily basis, which means we will have to listen a lot more and talk a lot less.

As friends of Christ, we must hear His voice not only in order to know *what* to pray, but also to know *when* to pray. So often our prayer lives become little more than a litany of people's needs, many of which we have no idea how God wants to meet, or even if He is calling us to stand in that particular gap. Over the past several years I have found myself increasingly overwhelmed by prayer-request overload. Not only does it seem there are constant calls to join this prayer chain or that special focus, but hardly a day goes by that I don't receive an e-mail asking prayer for someone I've never met. These are not trite needs—people's very lives and ministries may be on the line.

How can we possibly know what to pray, or even when, given this unanticipated outcome of the technological revolution? Do we join the group in our community that cries out for revival or the local Moms in Touch, or both? Do we participate in the thirty-day Muslim prayer focus or the 10/40-Window intercession emphasis or the forty-day Lenten fast for America's cities, or all of these, or none? Which of the 746,000 Web sites that turn up under an Internet search of the word *intercession* do we visit regularly?

In all seriousness, the way in which God is saturating our lives and Christian culture with opportunities to pray is a wonderful thing. I don't begrudge a single group or individual who makes their needs known for prayer to me via e-mail, the Web, or monthly newsletters. I can honestly say that I love it all. But I've learned that I can faithfully intercede for only those things God clearly places on my heart. Day by day, as I draw near and listen to His voice, I find out His plans for me in intercession and know that therein lies my joy.

FACE-TO-FACE

Moses, the great intercessor of the Old Testament, not only listened to God's voice, but Scripture says God actually spoke to him "face to face, just as a man speaks to his friend" (Exodus 33:11).

Though we don't know exactly what this meant, we can be sure that because God viewed Moses as His friend, He chose to manifest His presence to him in unique and blessed ways. The result was that Moses came to know God perhaps better than any human being ever has.

Of course it wasn't always so. The first time Moses met God at the burning bush, he knew almost nothing about Him, having been raised in the pagan Egyptian culture. When I AM told him that He was the God of Abraham, Isaac, and Jacob, Moses was so terrified that he couldn't even look up (Exodus 3). You might say the next year was a crash course for Moses in getting to know the God of his ancestors in a personal way. From resisting Yahweh's call to lead the Israelites out of bondage to watching his staff slither like a snake at his feet, from the plagues in Egypt to the extraordinary escape through the Red Sea, from wanderings in the wilderness to his forty-day stint on Mount Sinai—all of these experiences were teaching Moses firsthand what God was like.

That's why, when he stood in the gap for the Israelites over the golden calf incident, Moses knew exactly how to pray. Reminding God of His promise to Abraham, Moses's prayer burned like a laser beam through the heart of a covenant-keeping God, causing Him to relent, as Moses knew it would. For the next several months, the two of them communed regularly in the Tent of Meeting outside the camp. All the people knew the encounters in that place were sacred—men, women, and children would wait expectantly at the flaps of their own tents until Moses came out, the glory of the Lord beaming from his countenance.

I believe one of these interchanges reveals why God considered Moses such a dear friend. When God told him that instead of His presence an angel would now accompany the Israelites to the Promised Land, Moses balked. Though God assured him that a celestial being could guide them, meet all their needs, and perform whatever miracles were necessary, Moses didn't care—he wanted God or he wasn't going. Here was a man who held the future of more than a million people in his hands, a leader with unsurpassed power and influence, yet for Moses, none of this could compare to the treasure he'd come to know in walking intimately with God.

God's answer was swift and poignant: "I will indeed do what you have asked, for you have found favor with me, and you are my friend" (Exodus 33:17 NLT). Now at this point, had it been me, I think I would have breathed a sigh of relief, patted myself on the back, and gone off to marshal the troops. Not so with Moses. Seemingly oblivious to anything else, he pressed in almost to the point of being pushy and asked God to show him His glory one more time.

Can you see what is going on here? This man had enjoyed an amazing level of intimacy with God. Because he experienced something of Jehovah's magnificence each time they met face-to-face, these rendezvous had become the driving force behind all that Moses did. This is why getting answers to prayer would never have been enough for Moses, though he'd experienced stupendous success in intercession. Through all their wilderness wanderings, this friend of God found his greatest joy in moments when he happened to get one more glimpse of His glory.

As contemplative intercessors, we—like Moses—treasure our relationships as friends of God, never losing a sense of awe that He desires to reveal Himself to us. Every taste of His glory only spurs us to know Him more. When our intercessions are formed in this place of intimate knowledge, we pray with a conscious awareness that we are in pursuit of our greatest goal—to see God's glory manifested in hearts and lives and communities and cities and nations and to the ends of the earth. What a holy, blessed privilege.

THE BIG *D* WORD

I want to end this chapter with a few thoughts on the issue of discipline as it relates to intimacy and intercession. I've waited till now to mention this, because most people I talk to about prayer already feel a measure of guilt and some fear of failure. The last thing they need is someone telling them to be more diligent. Yet, at the same time, we all know that without discipline our best intentions often go by the wayside. For me, the question is not whether we need discipline, but how we can know whether we're grinding something out in our own strength or whether the work we're investing is, as Paul put it, "the grace of God with me" (1 Corinthians 15:10).

To answer that, let's imagine a real-life scenario. Suppose you want to start praying more intentionally for your neighbors and have decided to block out ten minutes for this in your morning quiet time each day. The first morning things seem to go okay, but on the second you are distracted by other situations the entire time. The third morning you are overwhelmed by the needs in your own family, and by the fourth you are frustrated with your lack of faith and wonder what difference ten minutes could possibly make anyway.

Do you stop trying at this point and wait until some special "intercession anointing" descends that will throw you with passion into the prayer closet? I wish it were that simple. Experienced intercessors will say that their spiritual lives have not been formed without hard decisions to obey when neither the desire nor the faith was quite there. Even Paul, who enjoyed some astounding experiences in God's presence, said he had to discipline his own body to make it his slave (1 Corinthians 9:27).

But what I want to suggest is that we must do more than just dig in and determine to work harder. Discipline by itself is meaningless—every other religion in the world does a good job of producing it. What we need is to renew our vision of why we intercede. We're not trying to earn anything from God or make ourselves more spiritual or get a job done. We are in pursuit of the only thing that can truly satisfy our souls, which is to know Jesus and make Him known. I've found three questions that can help me in this process:

1. Am I motivated by joy?
2. Am I spurred on by love?
3. Am I relishing my relationship as a needy child with the heavenly Father?

Let's start with the joy issue. Unless delight in the Lord is at the heart of our prayer lives, we will find ourselves laboring under a form of legalism instead of grace. Obviously this doesn't mean that giddy experiences will accompany our times of intercession (although that can certainly happen).

Sometimes we may not feel anything at all, but for the joy set before us, we're willing to do what it takes.

It's kind of like when I joined a gym several years ago. I remember many early mornings when I had to force myself to get dressed and get into the car to go. Every step of the way was hard work, but I knew that in the end I'd be glad if I just persevered. The amazing thing now, several years later, is that I love the whole experience—I can't imagine it not being a part of my life.

In the same way, growing in intercession sometimes requires taking steps that may seem more work than joy at first. But when that happens, we need to remind ourselves that we're after something wonderful: seeing more of Jesus manifested in the lives of others. This is what makes the tough work worthwhile.

Another test concerns whether we are serving God out of the overflow of love in our hearts. If we begin to feel weighted down by the needs of others or under some heavy load about our prayer lives in general, we may have lost our sense of wonder at God's love for us and for others. Jesus said that love would produce obedience to His commands, and as John reminded the early church, His "commandments are not burdensome" (1 John 5:3). Though the Lord may give us some intense situations to carry in prayer, if we are walking by His grace, even those will feel light, for His yoke is easy. If this is not the case, we may need to return to the simplicity of what it means to be in love with Jesus and, from that place, pursue the discipline we need.

Finally, we need to test ourselves to see if we are relishing our relationship as needy children with a good and generous Father. When we are seeking greater discipline in intercession and begin to feel discouraged over our weaknesses or doubt that we'll ever "get it right," we're most likely expecting more from ourselves than we can ever deliver. When this happens, our tendency is actually to walk away from God rather than run to Him.

The truth is that we all are needy children, and by embracing instead of resisting this, we'll have a much greater opportunity to see God go to work on our behalf. It has taken me years to really comprehend that God doesn't stand with pointed finger and disgusted frown when I fail, but instead He beckons me to come to Him for help. Scripture says, among other things, that God will deliver the needy, that He stands at the right hand of the needy, hears the needy, sets the needy securely on high, lifts the needy from the ash heap, and has compassion on the needy.[3]

Believing this changes our focus in discipline. When we're frustrated by our inconsistency, we'll throw ourselves upon God's mercy to do the work in us we need to change. Instead of feeling guilty about our selfishness and lack of compassion for the needs of others, we'll cry out for His Spirit to give us the desire we can't conjure up. Instead of getting discouraged when we see how wishy-washy we are in our commitment to pray, we'll call upon God, who alone can give us a greater grace.

I find it helpful to do this kind of an attitude check on a regular basis. There are times when I have to set aside my attempts at discipline in order to seek God's face as to why

> Whether it feels like it or not, there is profound joy in being used of God to bring the beauty of Christ to bear on the needs of the world.

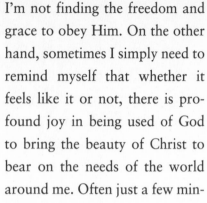

I'm not finding the freedom and grace to obey Him. On the other hand, sometimes I simply need to remind myself that whether it feels like it or not, there is profound joy in being used of God to bring the beauty of Christ to bear on the needs of the world around me. Often just a few minutes in quiet reflection on God's love and my own need for grace will fill me with fresh desire to do the hard work necessary for growth in this area.

Let me end these thoughts on discipline with a practical suggestion that, although it may seem rather obvious, I think needs to be said. For each of us, the best place to begin is right where we are. I believe one of Satan's greatest strategies is to dissuade us by setting such a high standard in front of us that we give up before we get started. The people who write the books we read on intercession have usually spent a lifetime learning the craft, but we forget that and think we ought to be like them right now. The truth is they didn't get there overnight—they have been on a journey and struggled with the same weaknesses and failures you and I face every day. To resist taking steps forward because we feel the ultimate goal is out of our reach is like not wanting to hike the mountain trail in our community because we fear we could never climb Mount Everest. Ask the Lord to guide you in setting one simple goal for growth in intercession and then, just do it. You'll be so glad you did.

INTIMATE INTERCESSION

Though I have tried throughout this chapter to make the case that intercession is more about intimacy than getting results, the truth is that God does answer prayer. Frankly, I sometimes wonder if He isn't amazed when we go on day after day, oblivious to how He wants to use us as intercessors. He once told Ezekiel, "I searched for a man among them who would build up the wall and stand in the gap before Me for the land, so that I would not destroy it; but I found no one" (Ezekiel 22:30). The book of Isaiah tells of a similar time when God was astonished that no one was available to intercede, but then Isaiah added these significant words: "Then His own arm brought salvation to Him" (59:16).

Here's the amazing thing: God wants to use us in prayer and He intends to use us in prayer, though He does not need to do so, as we've already seen. His own arm can bring about the results with just a thought in the right direction. Yet the Maker of heaven and earth longs to share His heart with us, letting us walk with Him and work with Him for the sake of His glorious name.

Isaiah wrote, "The Lord GOD has given Me the tongue of disciples, that I may know how to sustain the weary one with a word. He awakens Me morning by morning, He awakens My

Though it takes time to sit at His feet and practice to recognize His voice, intimacy in intercession can be one of the most exciting ventures we will ever embrace as servants of the Lord.

ear to listen as a disciple" (50:4). This is the life of a contemplative intercessor—awakening each day fully aware of the possibilities that come from hearing what God has to say and then joining Him in touching our world through prayer.

Can you see Him there, canvas spread out, brush in hand, just waiting for you to stand close, where He can include you in the creation of marvelous masterpieces involving hearts and lives and families and churches and communities and even nations? Though it takes time to sit at His feet and practice to recognize His voice, intimacy in intercession can be one of the most exciting ventures we will ever embrace as servants of the Lord. Why would we ever resist?

PRACTICING PRAYER

Once again we will pause to meditate on the prayers of other saints. Here's a format you can follow, but feel free to establish your own:

- Read these prayers silently through once, pondering the heart and meaning in them.
- Read each one aloud, as if it were your own.
- Journal your thoughts about what you have read, then write your own prayer.
- Read your written prayer to the Lord aloud.

A PRAYER OF NEHEMIAH
FOR JERUSALEM
(NEHEMIAH 1:5–11 NLT)

O LORD, God of heaven, the great and awesome God who keeps his covenant of unfailing love with those who love him and obey his commands, listen to my prayer! Look down and see me praying night and day for your people Israel. I confess that we have sinned against you. Yes, even my own family and I have sinned! We have sinned terribly by not obeying the commands, laws, and regulations that you gave us through your servant Moses.

Please remember what you told your servant Moses: "If you sin, I will scatter you among the nations. But if you return to me and obey my commands, even if you are exiled to the ends of the earth, I will bring you back to the place I have chosen for my name to be honored."

We are your servants, the people you rescued by your great power and might. O Lord, please hear my prayer! Listen to the prayers of those of us who delight in honoring you. Please grant me success now as I go to ask the king for a great favor. Put it into his heart to be kind to me.

A PRAYER OF CLEMENT OF ROME (FIRST CENTURY)

Clement, possibly mentioned in Philippians 4:3, was one of the earliest converts to Christianity and probably knew Christ or Paul personally. As bishop of Rome in the first century, he wrote a letter to the church at Corinth, which ended with the first prayer below. (We don't know the circumstances behind the second.)

First Prayer
> May God, who seeth all things,
> and who is the Ruler of all spirits and the Lord of
>   all flesh—
> who chose our Lord Jesus Christ and us through
>   Him to be a peculiar people—
> grant to every soul that calleth upon His glorious
>   and holy Name,
> faith, fear, peace, patience, long-suffering, self-
>   control, purity, and sobriety,
> to the well-pleasing of His Name,
> through our High Priest and Protector, Jesus Christ,
> by whom be to Him glory, and majesty, and power,
>   and honor,
> both now and forevermore.
> Amen.

Second Prayer

> We beseech thee, Master, to be our helper and
> protector.
>
> Save the afflicted among us; have mercy on the lowly;
>
> raise up the fallen; appear to the needy; heal the
> ungodly;
>
> restore the wanderers of thy people;
>
> feed the hungry; ransom our prisoners;
>
> raise up the sick; comfort the faint-hearted.

LOOKING AHEAD

Intimacy with Christ that is formed in the quiet place inevitably impacts every aspect of our lives. When intercession springs from this kind of relationship with God, it breaks out of the narrow confines of an activity or exercise and permeates all we do. Jesus showed us what this could look like through the way He lived on this earth in communion with His Father. In the next chapter we will learn from His example of an interceding life, and what this means for us on a very practical basis. And remember—Jesus, the great Intercessor, is praying for *you* this very moment.

CHAPTER FOUR

THE INTERCEDING LIFE

---

*Fulfilling Our Destiny
as Intercessors*

---

*Christ is not sitting passively in blissful
royal-dignity, unmoved, while you intercede. No! Never! You intercede because
He intercedes. The Holy Spirit conveys
to you the heartbeat of Jesus. You feel
but the faintest burden of concern as
compared with the infinite concern that
Jesus feels for you and with you.*

WESLEY DUEWEL[1]

O ne thing we know for sure about this world . . .
the known inhabited world is Flat, Level, a Plain
World." These were the words of Charles Johnson,
president of the Flat Earth Society until his death in 2001.[2]
Mr. Johnson was convinced that scientists throughout history had conspired to deceive the masses into believing the
world was round. When NASA's amazing photos of planet
Earth from deep space began to circulate, the Flat Earth
Society put out a bulletin explaining that the *Apollo* moon
landing was an elaborate Hollywood hoax scripted by a
famous sci-fi writer of the day. For nearly thirty years
Charles Johnson fought tenaciously to, as he put it, "restore
the world to sanity."

How can anyone in the twenty-first century still cling to
the notion that the earth is flat, given the inordinate amount
of evidence to the contrary? What causes someone to so
bury his head in the sand that he simply cannot accept reality? To understand the perspective of Charles and his wife,

Marjorie, I believe we need go no farther than the view from their front door.

A reporter who interviewed the couple discovered that their California home was surrounded by an incredible panorama of the Mojave Desert, as flat as a pancake for as far as the eye could see. From their vantage point, the idea of a spherical earth simply made no sense. Marjorie, who had come to the United States from Australia, even felt compelled to swear in an affidavit that she had never hung from her feet there, which is what she believed would have been necessary had it truly been the "land down under." To the Johnsons, the earth was flat, period, and nothing anyone might say or do could change their flawed outlook.

When it comes to a life of intercession, I feel at times a bit like these flat-earth folks. Although it is an established fact that I am seated with Christ in heavenly places, day after day I look out my window and instead choose to live by what I see in front of my eyes. I watch the five young men move in across the street, for example, and fret over the potential loss in property value, instead of considering that God put them there that I might stand in the gap on their behalf. I read the grades on my son's report card and find myself fussing and fuming, instead of pondering how God might want to use these difficulties to hone my son's heart and mine as I lift him up in prayer.

Here's the truth: Intercession is a language for the Spirit realm, and to the degree that our sights are set on what is taking place in front of our eyes, we will find little use for it. To embrace an interceding life we must become adept at being in this world, but not of it, at looking at what is unseen instead of what is seen (John 17:13–21; 2 Corinthians 4:18). When we do, we will find that prayer is no longer an activity to engage in from time to time, but something that saturates every aspect of our lives.

Jesus did this perfectly. When He entered this earth, He took on flesh and blood, struggling throughout His life with the same weaknesses you and I face, yet somehow managing to walk in continual communion with His Father. The disciples were so intrigued by this that it was the one thing they asked Him to teach them directly. My desire for this chapter is that their words "Lord, teach us to pray" would become our own plea as we begin to grasp the principles that governed Christ's actions and the convictions that shaped His world-view.

AS SIMPLE AS BEING A BRANCH

Over the past few years, we have been working to turn our backyard and the hill behind it into a prayer garden. Because the area is sun-splattered for most of the day, we bought one very large tree for shade. Several months after we planted it, we noticed that the trunk was leaning toward our house and realized that if we didn't do something, it was going to be a problem down the road. So, with the help of some strong young men, my husband looped heavy wire around the tree and tugged until the trunk was straight, fastening the wire to some pegs that they'd pounded into the ground a few feet away. Because the tree still seemed prone

The Holy Spirit within us is not only a personal prayer trainer, but a prayer warrior in His own right, doing what comes naturally, which is to pray.

to pull the other way, we had to tighten the line by an inch or two on several occasions over the next few months.

One day as I sat on a bench nearby and noticed its slight lean once again, it occurred to me that the branches of the tree really had nothing to do with the whole thing. Whether that trunk stood upright or inclined itself in the direction of my house, those leafy appendages had no say—they just kept right on casting their shade for me to enjoy. Now this was no great epiphany or anything, but as I looked up, I thought of Jesus's words— "I am the vine, you are the branches" (John 15:5)—and it all suddenly seemed so simple.

Being a branch means just that—being a branch. No truth is more critical to the interceding life than this one. When Jesus said He would send another Helper to be with us and in us, He used the word *paracletos*, which literally meant one who would plead the cause of another or, in other words, an intercessor![3] It is a freeing truth that the Holy Spirit within us is not only a personal prayer trainer, but a prayer warrior in His own right, doing what comes naturally, which is to pray. Like that trunk on my fruitless mulberry, Jesus not only determines the direction we should go, but has the strength to bring us along. We're just branches, drawing everything we need to intercede from Him.

This is the solution for those times when we feel inept at

intercession or even lack the motivation to pray. Affirming that the Spirit has come to set up housekeeping within our hearts, we cling to the promise: "In the same way the Spirit also helps our weakness; for we do not know how to pray as we should, but the Spirit Himself intercedes for us" (Romans 8:26). In his simple yet profound treatise on prayer, O. Hallesby wrote:

> As long as we measure our power to pray persistently and in the right way, by what we feel or think we can accomplish, we shall be discouraged when we hear of how much we ought to pray. But when we quietly believe that the Holy Spirit as a Spirit of supplication is dwelling within us in the middle of all our conscious weakness, for the very purpose of enabling us to pray in such manner and measure as God would have us, our hearts are filled with hope.[4]

You see? Instead of feeling pressured to master methods or stir up zeal as intercessors, we need only welcome the Holy Spirit like a dear friend, seeking daily to make Him a home in our hearts.

This is far more attainable than we might think. Just recognizing that the Holy Spirit loves to pray through us can cause us to see things differently. For example, when we walk into

Instead of feeling pressured to master methods or stir up zeal as intercessors, we need only welcome the Holy Spirit like a dear friend.

church and spot someone across the auditorium who then weighs heavily on our minds throughout the service, we realize that this is the Spirit prompting us to pray for them. When we drive down the street and the image of a young mother walking with her children stays with us for the next few minutes, we grasp that we are being granted an opportunity to intercede for them.

This is so simple we can miss it. I believe each of us would pray a lot more if we just realized that the Spirit's heart of intercession is always beating within us. This takes us away from a sort of utilitarian approach to prayer (doing it for the results alone) and moves us into a way of life that is, frankly, a lot of fun. When we live with a conscious awareness that the interceding Spirit indwells each of us, we'll take great delight in being like archers who send His arrows of prayer zinging toward their targets day in and day out.

Take, for example, my own neighborhood. We have lived here for eighteen years and have seen a lot of families move in and out during that time. Though I would love to see a great move of God here and have asked for that many times, so far it hasn't happened. But what has taken place is that I've had the opportunity to lift up a number of families I may never see again in prayer. Most of the time, this has involved short, simple requests as I've listened to God's voice and tried to express what I think is on His heart. On occasion, the Spirit has burdened me in a deeper way, leading to a more extended season of intercession. Though I cannot claim great visible results in many of the cases, I am confident that God has a purpose in everything I've prayed.

Another amazing thing about the Spirit's praying in us is that we don't even have to worry that we'll pray the wrong thing when we stand in the gap for others: "He who searches the hearts knows what the mind of the Spirit is, because He intercedes for the saints according to the will of God" (Romans 8:27). Isn't this great? The Spirit looks past our bumbling attempts to say the right thing or pray the right prayer and sees what is in our hearts. As we abide in Christ, He promises to intercede for us according to God's will, however inadequate our notions of the need at hand might be.

IN CONTINUAL COMMUNION WITH OUR FATHER

Jesus demonstrated the two aspects of being a branch—our abiding in Him and His abiding in us—through His earthly relationship with His Father, whether communing with Him in seasons of private prayer or right in the midst of a bustling crowd. One of my favorite examples is the time Jesus was unleashing a tirade of woes against unrepentant cities, when suddenly He seemed to switch gears, letting His audience in on a personal conversation that must have been going on with His Father at the same time. The Scripture says, "At that time Jesus said, 'I praise You, Father, Lord of heaven and earth, that You have hidden these things from the wise and intelligent and have revealed them to infants'" (Matthew 11:25). Then, without missing a beat, Jesus turned back to the crowd to finish His exhortation to them.

I remember the first time I met someone who seemed to

> To commune with God as Jesus did means that though the physical realm may be in our faces, the spiritual realm is always right there in our peripheral vision.

live like this. During conversations, this woman would often look off in the distance for a minute and then turn back and share some word from the Lord. When she and her husband came to our house for a meal, my teenage son came through the door, and she immediately engaged him in a private thirty-minute conversation concerning the things that she sensed were on God's heart for him. I have never been with her in a group that she didn't at some point call us all to stop and see if God had anything to say.

The woman's name was Joy Dawson, one of the founding "mothers" of YWAM and a mentor and role model to thousands of intercessors across the world. When I met her, I honestly thought she was an aberration, for I'd never met a Christian who took Scripture's admonition to pray without ceasing so literally. Joy's life reflected constant communion with God as she listened for His voice in even the smallest details. Though I was filled with awe whenever I was with her, I couldn't imagine that this was something an average believer like myself might experience on a consistent basis.

Now, several years later, I know that though she was an exceptionally godly woman, the kind of intimacy Joy demonstrated with Christ is not only something to which we all can aspire, but something He desires for each of us. Though I am nowhere near as adept at hearing God or even remembering to stop and listen for Him to speak, I am growing in that grace day by day and finding delight in the process.

Recently I heard a pastor compare this kind of walk with God to picture-in-picture (PIP) televisions, where one program can be viewed on the entire screen while another is superimposed on a much smaller scale in the screen's corner. To commune with God as Jesus did means that though the physical realm may be in our faces, the spiritual realm is always right there in our peripheral vision. Not only has God given us the ability to engage in both at the same time, but He has made our spiritual lives to depend upon it.

This is why Jesus could say, "Truly, truly, I say to you, the Son can do nothing of Himself, unless it is something He sees the Father doing; for whatever the Father does, these things the Son also does in like manner. For the Father loves the Son, and shows Him all things that He Himself is doing" (John 5:19–20). The direction of Christ's days was formed in communion with His Father concerning the things He could see were already taking place in the heavenlies. Wouldn't you love for this to be your testimony as well? For intercession to be more like tapping into the workings of the Maker of the universe than a series of dutiful requests?

Several mornings a week, my husband and I have a short prayer time in which we interact with God over various situations in our lives. Whether interceding for our church, our children, or our lost neighbors, we ask God first what is taking place in the unseen realm and what is on His heart for a given situation. For example, today we prayed for our oldest son and his family, who recently moved to another state

Here is the stunning truth that ought to make our hearts beat a little faster: Jesus has given us the keys to the kingdom!

to start a new business. As parents, we are prone to pray in a certain way ("Make them bring our grandchildren back, Lord"), but what does God want? Though Scripture is full of specific things we could pray, how do we know which verses apply right now to their situation? Is their greatest need to prosper and be in good health or to learn obedience through suffering? Is it to experience the immeasurable love of God or to learn how to walk by faith and not sight? What is God doing in them, and how can this best be accomplished?

The more we learn to engage with God's heart, the greater our confidence that He will grant the things for which we ask. "This is the confidence which we have before Him, that, if we ask anything according to His will, He hears us" (1 John 5:14). By moving beyond sharing our own ideas and desires for others with the Lord to actually interacting over the plan He reveals to us and then praying on that basis, we find our faith increasing and intercession becoming a lot more exciting. As Joy Dawson says, communing with God like this ruins us for the ordinary.[5] I have to agree.

WITH ZEAL FOR HIS KINGDOM

Jesus's favorite description of the spiritual realm in which He and His Father communed seemed to be the "kingdom of

God" or the "kingdom of heaven." More than any other subject, stories about the kingdom dominated private discussions Jesus had with His disciples. In His first recorded public sermon, Jesus exhorted listeners to make His kingdom the centerpiece of their lives, promising that His Father would take care of all their other needs as a result (Matthew 6:33).[6]

The kingdom of God was precious to Christ, like a pearl of great price. He continually made it clear that life in this realm was worth leaving everything for. When some would-be followers wanted to say good-bye to their families before joining Him, Jesus said that if they had to look back, they weren't fit for the kingdom. He insisted that the rewards of the kingdom far exceeded the losses of those who were forced to leave family or friends or houses or lands in order to follow Him.[7]

The interceding life is one that shares Christ's appreciation for the value of His kingdom—not only as our final destiny, but as an inheritance to enjoy daily. Though we live with eager anticipation of that moment when every knee will bow before Christ, we don't have a pie-in-the-sky ambivalence or disdain for life on this earth. The more we taste of the glory of Christ's reign in our own hearts, the more we yearn to see it established on this planet where demons gloat and the people around us suffer the agonizing effects of sin's domain.

Here is the stunning truth that ought to make our hearts beat a little faster: Jesus has given us the keys to the kingdom! He taught Peter and the disciples that because they held these keys, they would be able to bind on earth what is already bound in heaven and to loose on earth what is already loosed in heaven (Matthew 16:19; 18:18). Later, when He repeated this promise, Jesus added: "Again I say to you, that if two of you agree on earth about anything that they may ask, it shall be done for them by My Father who is in heaven" (Matthew 18:19).

Not only are we as citizens to enjoy the kingdom's benefits from here to eternity, but we can be channels of its bounty to a world still imprisoned by darkness and despair. Like kids in a candy store, we have the means to open the door and share the goods with those on the outside. We can bring healing to the sick, comfort to the brokenhearted, hope to the despairing, wisdom to the confused, deliverance to the oppressed, peace to the troubled, and kindness to the down-and-out.

Think of it! We can wake up every morning with assurance that the keys to the kingdom belong to us—we don't even have to go looking for them! Throughout our day, we can feel them there reminding us of our heritage, like a set of keys jingling in our pockets assures us of our access to a home or a car or the office in which we work. We can unlock the storehouse of heaven—once a day or a hundred times a day—in a breath of prayer here or a desperate cry there, in seasons of wee-hour weeping or declarations of faith on the run. And every night as we go to sleep, we can look back, knowing that the kingdom of God has indeed come, even if in small increments.

Knowing this ought to make us the most hope-filled people on the planet, yet often it doesn't. Why? Because we forget, or perhaps have never really understood, that there is only one set of keys that can open heaven's gates. Instead of praying, we sweat and strive and structure our world with Christian activity. Instead of interceding, we work and plan and build programs that lack God's transforming power. We breathe a weary sigh as we go to bed, wondering where we'll get the energy to keep working for a kingdom whose keys are buried beneath a mound of busyness.

As newlyweds, my husband and I learned what an incomparable asset the keys to the kingdom were while serving as missionaries in a small Eskimo village. We had left home bright-eyed and optimistic, harboring lofty visions of success and a confidence that all one hundred or so Eskimos would easily be saved in our two-year stint there. (Trust me—this was more youthful naiveté than faith.)

Our first day there brought a rude awakening as we stood in our small cabin surrounded by curious children and realized that we didn't have a clue about what we were doing. The villagers watched us warily from the start, not willing to entrust themselves to a couple of young white kids fresh out of college. All our ideas and plans meant nothing to a people who seemed to have little interest in Christianity. We soon found ourselves lonely and confused, wondering if we could accomplish anything at all for the kingdom in that place.

Out of desperation we wrote everyone we knew, asking for prayer. My grandmother responded with much-needed wisdom. Having homesteaded land in the hills of Alabama with my grandfather, she knew a lot about farming and soil. Her letter told of how growing cotton was the easiest part of the job, whereas getting the soil ready was the real work. They

They would have to first till the soil, soak it, then till it and soak it again until it was soft enough to fold in fertilizer to feed the precious cottonseeds they would sow.

would have to first till the soil, soak it, then till it and soak it again until it was soft enough to fold in fertilizer to feed the precious cottonseeds they would sow. When I read her words, I began to see our two-year assignment in a very different light. I knew that no matter what else we might do with our time there, intercession was the real work needed if the kingdom was ever to take root in the soil of those hardened Eskimo hearts.

To be zealous for the kingdom as Christ was means first and foremost to be a person of prayer. These are the keys He has given us, and though opening heaven's doors may not always happen as quickly as we want, the joy of being a kingdom seeker makes it worth the wait. Can you hear Him encouraging you even now? "Do not be afraid, little flock, for your Father has chosen gladly to give you the kingdom" (Luke 12:32). God delights to hear and answer our prayers, so that the wonders of His Son's reign might come to our sons and daughters, our sisters and brothers, our neighbors and teachers and students and leaders and car mechanics and pastors—yes, especially our pastors.

LAYING DOWN OUR LIVES

God is always blessed when we choose to pray for others, but I believe there are times in intercession when, if we were to stop and listen, we might hear sighs of pleasure coming from the throne of our happy God. Consider this: God the Father is ever enthralled with the beauty of His Son, who laid down His life to bridge the gap between Himself and sinful humanity. When praying for others requires that we die as well—to our own needs, desires, rights, and even our hopes and dreams—we have the opportunity to reflect the merciful heart of Jesus, who ever lives to make intercession for sinners, something that gives God immense pleasure.

Jesus's commitment to identify with broken people cost Him His life, and, as intercessors, if we would take up our crosses and follow Him, we will pay a price as well, something Brennan Manning calls the "mandatory crucifixion of the ego."[8] Let's face it—there's little glory in interceding for those who may never even know about it or, if they do, just don't care. Beyond that, Jesus has commanded us to pray for people who are blatantly hostile or who say evil things about us. Herein lies the rub. How in the world do we intercede for others in the face of their oblivion or in-difference or even painful rejection? How, in fact, do we come to the place where we can gladly pray blessing even upon those who have cursed or persecuted us (Matthew 5:43–45)?

Our only recourse is to go to the foot of the cross and gaze upon the face of our Lord as He hangs there. Abandoned and betrayed by those dear to Him, rejected by the religious elite, assaulted by the taunts of mockers and scorned by drunken soldiers, He pleaded tenderly, "Father, forgive them, for they do not know what they are doing." By

enabling us to do as He did, Jesus extends to every intercessor the blessed privilege of sharing in the fellowship of His
sufferings, something that profoundly changes us and deeply
blesses the heart of God.⁹

On the shelf in my husband's office are two rocks the
size of a hand, a gift from an Indian pastor named Peter
Kashung, who tirelessly gives his life to bring the gospel to
tribes throughout northeast India. Peter often faces dangerous opposition, the story behind the rocks being one of
those times. On a sunny afternoon a few years ago, as Peter
preached before a crowd in the open air, some young men
from the nearby village began to heckle him. The longer he
preached, the louder they yelled. When that didn't deter
him, they began to pick up rocks and hurl them at him.
After getting hit numerous times, Peter finally stopped,
leaned down, and picked up each rock they'd thrown, plac-
ing them carefully in his bag. Then, looking directly at the
rabble-rousers, Peter spoke softly, promising that he would
put those rocks where he could see them every day, as a
reminder to pray for them. Shrugging their shoulders and
shaking their heads in disgust, the young men left.

We who live in a Western culture may never experience
the kinds of things Peter Kashung faces on a regular basis,
but our call is the same. The wounds we receive may be
inflicted not with stones, but with words that leave scars on
our souls rather than on our bodies. When this happens, we
have a choice. We can put up walls to hide our anger and
pain and resentment, or we can die to the flesh and gather
those words as Peter did the stones, using them as a reminder

to pray. Francis Frangipane calls this the gift of wounded-ness, for in it there is great gain:

> To be wounded in the service of mercy and, instead of closing our hearts, allow woundedness to crown love, is to release God's power in redemption. The steadfast prayer of the wounded intercessor holds great sway upon the heart of God.[10]

I experienced the mystery of this one time when I received an especially unkind e-mail from someone who had become disgruntled with our church. It had been a rough season in ministry, and few people knew the extent of our difficulties as the attacks against my husband and me seemed to come with increasing regularity. With each fresh assault, pain shot through my heart like an arrow.

As we sought the Lord, He made it clear that we were not to try to defend ourselves, but to trust Him with our anguish and pray for those whose words were wounding us. And so we did. But when that e-mail came, all I could think of was that if others could see what this person had written, they'd feel our hurt and perhaps extend some much-needed sympathy. Keenly aware as I sat there that this was not God's heart, I tried instead to pray for the person who had sent the e-mail. Unable to feel the desire or even know what to pray, I finally cried out, "Lord, no one knows how hard this is or how much I am suffering."

As quickly as that prayer escaped my lips, these words rang in my heart: *I know. I see every wound. And this is*

> When Jesus calls us to pray, He provides all we need in order to do so.

enough. I can't explain it, but the sweetness of the moments that followed far outweighed my hurt. From that point forward, every time another assault came, I knew that as I lifted that person up in prayer and asked God to bless them, He would manifest His tender presence to me, and I would be restored.

The awesome reward of the interceding life is just this: the pleasure of God poured out upon us as we meet with Him at the mercy seat in prayer for others. Following Jesus, who entered the holy place once for all through His own blood, we, too, lay down our lives and draw near with a sincere heart and full assurance of faith and, in so doing, move the heart of our heavenly Father (Hebrews 9:12; 10:22).

ALWAYS ENOUGH

Though intercession brings unique burdens at times and almost always mandates a death to selfish desire, when Jesus calls us to pray, He provides all we need in order to do so. This He has promised—the yoke we wear as intercessors is by its very nature easy, and the burden we carry light. He will never give us more than we can bear, for His grace is ever sufficient, a truth that must permeate the life of every person of prayer.

Jesus demonstrated this in a graphic way in the feeding of the five thousand. The event took place just after the disciples had returned from their first venture into kingdom ministry without Him. While they were regaling Him with tales of healing and deliverance, Jesus realized they hadn't even taken time to eat, so He suggested that they go someplace quiet and rest for a while. The thirteen of them climbed into a boat and set off, but they were to have no peaceful privacy. The crowds, watching the direction they had gone, ran ahead on foot, gathering friends along the way. By the time Jesus and the disciples arrived at their destination, a multitude awaited them.

When He saw the crowds, Scripture tells us Jesus felt deep compassion. Knowing that they were like sheep without a shepherd, He began to teach, not stopping until the hour was late and everyone was famished. When you consider the condition the disciples must have been in by then, you can't blame them for suggesting that the masses go into the villages and buy their own dinner. But Jesus wanted something more critical than food for hungry stomachs. He wanted His closest followers—these men who would soon form the nucleus of His church—to see the bounty of heaven and learn that when it comes to the needs of others, there is always enough (Mark 6).

As intercessors, we will enjoy exhilarating experiences of kingdom power in prayer. But there will also be times when we feel we just don't have anything else to give, when the burdens Christ calls us to bear seem too heavy to handle. Just when we think we're ready for a well-deserved rest, we'll be asked to intercede for a child dying of leukemia or a teenager wasted on drugs or a pastor suffering moral failure. These are the moments when Jesus would remind us of the feeding of the five thousand and assure us that in Him, there is always enough.

Heidi and Rolland Baker illustrate this beautifully through their work among the poorest of the poor in Mozambique. They began ministering there with nothing but a heart for Jesus and a run-down hellhole of an orphanage that no one wanted to manage anymore. Day after day they gave their lives away, bringing in children who had suffered every kind of abuse in an effort to stay alive. One day the Bakers discovered that scores of orphans made the local dump—a place of horrid squalor—their home. Heidi and Rolland added this to their list of ministry spots, regularly visiting there to deliver food and clothing and to pray over child after child as they poured out the love of Christ. The work was endless and often overwhelming, death threats were common, and disease threatened their family at every point. Working eighteen-hour days, they ministered tirelessly to these fatherless children that everyone, including the African people, continued to tell them were not worth trying to save.

Finally the responsibilities of ministry grew too great, and Heidi began to get sick. Caring for more than three hundred children in their orphanage had worn her out, leaving her vulnerable to infection and dysentery and eventually inflicting her with a serious case of pneumonia. Terribly ill and unable to fight off sickness anymore, she had no choice but to withdraw for a season. After a short hospital stay, Heidi decided to leave the country and spend some time with a church in Canada where she knew God was moving mightily. Immediately upon her arrival, God began to bring miraculous physical healing and spiritual rest by pouring out His presence upon her day after day in the worship services there.

One night as Heidi groaned before the Lord in intercession for the children of Mozambique, something happened that would change her ministry and her life forever. She began to envision thousands of needy children, all coming toward her. Crying out, she started to tell the Lord no, there were just too many. In Heidi's own words, here is what happened next:

Then I had a dramatic, clear vision of Jesus. I was with Him, and thousands and thousands of children surrounded us. I saw His shining face and His intense, burning eyes of love. I also saw His body. It was bruised and broken, and His side was pierced. He said, "Look into My eyes. You give them something to eat." Then He took a piece of His broken body and handed it to me. It became bread in my hands, and I began to give it to the children. It multiplied in my hands. Then again the Lord said, "Look into My eyes. You give them something to drink." He gave me a cup of blood and water, which flowed from His side. I knew it was a cup of bitterness and joy. I drank it and then began to give it to the children to drink. The cup did not go dry. By this point I was crying uncontrollably. I was completely undone by His fiery eyes of love. I realized what it had cost Him to provide such spiritual and physical food for us all. The Lord spoke to my heart and said, "There will always be enough, because I died."[11]

> God has a very specific call for every intercessor, and He will reveal it to us, usually one need at a time.

Heidi shared how, from then on, they stopped seeing the vast poverty and destruction around them and instead began to look into the face of each child. By faith, they trusted that there would be enough for that one child's need—whether it be salvation or a home or clothing or health or school or simply a loving hug. When I read this, I thought of Mother Teresa, who often said that her worldwide ministry really began with one dying woman on the streets of India. She wrote:

> I never look at the masses as my responsibility. I look only at the individual. I can love only one person at a time. I can feed only one person at a time. Just one, one, one. So you begin . . . I begin . . . The whole work is only a drop in the ocean. But if we don't put the drop in, the ocean would be one drop less. Same thing for you. Same thing in your family. Same thing in the church where you go. Just begin . . . one, one, one.[12]

God has a very specific call for every intercessor, and He will reveal it to us, usually one need at a time. And though the people on whose behalf we pray may not seem as desperate as the poverty-stricken orphans in Mozambique or the people with leprosy on the streets of India, our ministry is the same. We follow the heart of Jesus to the destitute, the needy, the hurting, and the lost—whether it be our own prodigal child, a neighbor facing divorce, the migrant worker waiting for a job on the corner, or some remote tribe across the globe. One by one, we offer them up in prayer. And each time we intercede, if we will take the time to look into the eyes of Christ, we will understand in a deeper way that His body has been broken and His blood has been shed for them. And because He died, there will always be enough.

PRACTICING PRAYER

Once again we will pause to meditate on the prayers of other saints. Here's a format you can follow, but feel free to establish your own:

- Read these prayers silently through once, pondering the heart and meaning in them.
- Read each one aloud, as if it were your own.
- Journal your thoughts about what you have read, then write your own prayer.
- Read your written prayer to the Lord aloud.

A Prayer of Jesus for His Followers Before His Death
(John 17:1–26 nlt)

Father, the time has come. Glorify your Son so he can give glory back to you. For you have given him authority over everyone in all the earth. He gives eternal life to each one you have given him. And this is the way to have eternal life—to know you, the only true God, and Jesus Christ, the one you sent to earth. I brought glory to you here on earth by doing everything you told me to do. And now, Father, bring me into the glory we shared before the world began.

I have told these men about you. They were in the world, but then you gave them to me. Actually, they were always yours, and you gave them to me; and they have kept your word. Now they know that everything I have is a gift from you, for I have passed on to them the words you gave me; and they accepted them and know that I came from you, and they believe you sent me.

My prayer is not for the world, but for those you have given me, because they belong to you. And all of them, since they are mine, belong to you; and you have given them back to me, so they are my glory! Now I am departing the world; I am leaving them behind and coming to you. Holy Father, keep them and care for them—all those you have given me—so that they will be united just as we are. During my time here, I have kept them safe. I guarded them so that not one was lost, except the one headed for destruction, as the Scriptures foretold.

And now I am coming to you. I have told them many things while I was with them so they would be filled with my joy. I have given them your word. And the world hates them because they do not belong to the world, just as I do not. I'm not asking you to take them out of the world, but to keep them safe from the evil one. They are not part of this world any more than I am. Make them pure and holy by teaching them your words of truth. As you sent me into the world, I am sending them into the world. And I give myself entirely to you so they also might be entirely yours.

I am praying not only for these disciples but also for all who will ever believe in me because of their testimony. My prayer for all of them is that they will be one, just as you and I are one, Father—that just as you are in me and I am in you, so they will be in us, and the world will believe you sent me.

I have given them the glory you gave me, so that they may be one, as we are—I in them and you in me, all being perfected into one. Then the world will know that you sent me and will understand that you love them as much as you love me. Father, I want these whom you've given me to be with me, so they can see my glory. You gave me the glory because you loved me even before the world began!

O righteous Father, the world doesn't know you, but I do; and these disciples know you sent me. And I have revealed you to them and will keep on revealing you. I will do this so that your love for me may be in them and I in them.

A PRAYER OF AUGUSTINE OF HIPPO

Saint Augustine was a fourth-century church bishop and philosopher. His spiritual autobiography, Augustine's Confessions, *has had a major impact on Christian thought and practice.*

Watch Thou, dear Lord, with those who wake and
    watch or weep tonight,
and give thine angels charge over those who sleep.
    Tend Thy sick ones, O Lord Christ;
    rest Thy weary ones;
bless Thy dying ones;
    soothe Thy suffering ones;
    shield Thy joyous ones,
    and all for Thy Love's sake.

LOOKING AHEAD

Seeing the kingdom come through intercession is a life filled with joyful reward, but not without its difficulties. Jesus taught us that the kingdom must be seized with violent force, which is why spiritual warfare is such an integral part of what we do. In the next chapter we will discover who our enemies really are and how to fight the daily battles that are sure to come our way as we embrace the interceding life. I think you'll find that it's not nearly as complicated as you might have thought. In fact, establishing an effective prayer strategy for the war of the worlds can be an exhilarating challenge. Shall we jump into the fray?

CHAPTER FIVE

THERE'S A WAR GOING ON

Interceding from the Trenches of Life as We Know It

Prayer is indeed a continuous violent action of the spirit as it is lifted up to God. This action is comparable to that of a ship going against the stream.

MARTIN LUTHER[1]

The most profound treatise I've ever heard on prayer is summed up in two short lines that rhyme, although the author says he didn't realize it until he got up to preach on the subject. I should probably warn you that this fifteen-word ditty might not seem too impressive at first. It didn't to me—I thought it a bit corny, and the composition certainly didn't suggest the kinds of life-changing principles that have since shaped my Christian walk. Yet I can't think of a better way to begin a chapter on spiritual warfare, so here it is: "You will not know what prayer is for, until you know that life is war."[2]

That's it—the whole ball of wax. Of course in the message that followed, John Piper said all sorts of weighty things, as he is wont to do. But these few words stuck and, over time, birthed in me a new understanding of prayer and, particularly, intercession. Life is war. Though we may never fully grasp what took place when Satan and his armies were thrown to earth, the reality with which we must now reckon

"You will not know what prayer is for, until you know that life is war."

is that we are surrounded by spiritual forces of wickedness who take pleasure in wreaking destruction upon the children of the living God.

It is a clash of kingdoms we've been thrust into—the kingdom of darkness versus the kingdom of light. Our enemies are real. There are evil, diabolical beings that never give up trying to steal, kill, and destroy the work of Christ on this earth. Until we are consciously aware of this, we will not cling to prayer with the sort of fierce tenacity it warrants. We, as well as others for whom we intercede, are in a fight day in and day out. Prayer must permeate all we do, for no amount of activity—religious or otherwise—can withstand the level of firepower that Satan and his hosts continually launch against the purposes of God. *We will not know what prayer is for, until we know that life is war.*

WHAT ARE WE FIGHTING FOR?

As I write this chapter, the United States is engaged in a war that at times has seemed hard to imagine will ever come to an end. Like many others, I have often dreaded reading the paper or turning on the nightly news with its endless tales of bloodshed and death. From mounting casualties in roadside bombings to brutal beheadings and ill-equipped armed forces, there have been many days when things appeared about as bleak as they could be.

One week there was a press release about nineteen soldiers who had refused a convoy order because they felt the route was dangerous and they were not sufficiently protected to make the delivery of fuel to a town north of them. When I read this, I thought of the nature of war, of the sacrifices men and women have made throughout the centuries for a cause they felt was worthy of their lives. So what happened in this case? Why would a whole group of men and women who took an oath to defend their country simply refuse an order, something almost unheard of in military life?

I think the answer lies in a letter we recently received from a chaplain serving on the front lines. Here is some of what he wrote:

> In this war, we are not really sure what the definable objectives are that we are to reach . . . This is tough on soldiers. They are taught to go in and fight, win the objective, and secure an area. This deployment does not fit the normal war scenario for soldiers. It is hard for them to feel a sense of worth, accomplishment, or success. Remember these guys in your prayers. It has been hard on many seeing their buddies die each and every day and really not know what is going to happen. Will we win, will we stay, will we leave, are we just pawns for the politicians? Who knows?[3]

The problem these men and women faced is that as foot soldiers in the trenches they could not see the big picture and were confused about why they were there, or what it would mean to win the war. It's hard, as the chaplain says so poignantly, to lay down your own life or watch another die for a goal that is vague and indefinable, or for a cause whose success seems out of reach.

We face similar struggles with the spiritual warfare into which intercession often catapults us. We get lost in combat over one plot of ground, forgetting that ours is a small part in a much larger war. We battle in prayer over the needs of others, but we aren't sure what constitutes victory. If the answers do not come when we expect them or they look different from what we'd planned, we find ourselves discouraged and—like those soldiers—wonder why we are here anyway.

But there is a significant difference between the battles among men and those we face as intercessors. As citizens of a heavenly kingdom, we do know the big picture. We are fighting to see our King's reign extended across the planet that He created for His glory. In warfare large or small, our goal is to see Christ's kingdom come and His will be done on earth as it is in heaven. Jesus once explained how this works after He'd delivered a boy from a demon, causing no small amount of consternation among the Pharisees. Telling them that this was the finger of God bringing His kingdom, He went on to say:

> When a strong man, fully armed, guards his own house, his possessions are undisturbed. But when someone stronger than he attacks him and overpowers him, he

takes away from him all his armor on which he had relied and distributes his plunder. (Luke 11:21–22)

The reality we must grasp in prayer is that though Satan has been attacked, overpowered, and stripped of his armor, he is still holding on to a lot of plunder that isn't rightfully his. Through warfare intercession, we help others go in and get back the stuff in their lives that Jesus secured for His own purposes through His death and resurrection.

Though the battle may be fierce at times, we rejoice that there is no question about the final outcome in this war. Victory celebrations began the moment the Lamb of God cried out, "It is finished," from the cross of Calvary and made a public spectacle of His enemies (Colossians 2:15). When Christ rose, Satan and his hosts were forced at last to face the sobering reality that their power was limited and their time short.

Can you imagine what a difference this would make in any war effort—to know your outcome is secure? That no matter how bad things look, or how out of control they might seem, you can't possibly lose? This is no small thing—it directly impacts the way we view intercession. It's not up to us to win the war over the souls of men and women. Jesus has already done that. Our job is simply to report for duty when He calls and know that when we do, He

> When Christ rose, Satan and his hosts were forced at last to face the sobering reality that their power was limited and their time short.

delights to put us into service like millions of others who've joyfully fought throughout the centuries for His honor.

Storming about like a roaring lion, the evil one ever seeks to hold humanity hostage through fear and ignorance, but the gates of hell cannot prevail against Christ's church. All the rulers and powers and spiritual forces of wickedness in heavenly places will not keep us out. We are on the march, and whether we face a skirmish on the run or find ourselves dodging enemy troops in the thick of a knock-down drag-out, we sing a song of triumph, for we know the end of the story.

CAPTIVATED BY OUR KING

A serious approach to spiritual warfare requires something beyond the image of Christ that may be lodged in our minds as a relic of our Sunday school days. Gentle Jesus, meek and mild—as precious as this reality is—will not cut it when we are standing in the heat of battle where demons laugh as they launch missiles to blow up our prayers in midair. What we need is a vision of the exalted Christ, the same One who terrified John into a stupor on the Isle of Patmos. This Jesus—eyes piercing flames of fire, mouth wielding a two-edged sword, face shining so brightly that the sun looks dim by comparison—is the One we can be sure leads us into combat.[4]

He is the Captain of the hosts of heaven, a mighty Warrior riding forth on a white horse with all of His armies following behind. He is faithful and true, and He wages war in righteousness, fueled by His Father's fierce wrath against sin. All authority in heaven and on earth has been given to Christ, for He rides forth in majestic robes that have been dipped in His own blood. He is the King of kings and Lord of lords, so glorious that those who dwell in His presence can only fall on their faces before Him again and again as they cry out, "Holy, holy, holy is the Lord God almighty."[5]

Our Leader is the Lion of the tribe of Judah. He goes before us, holding high His banner of love while terrifying the hosts of hell so that we can fight for the glory of His name. As the consummate Commander in Chief, Christ determines the strategy of our warfare with perfect precision, for He is seated at the right hand of God, "far above all rule and authority and power and dominion, and every name that is named, not only in this age but also in the one to come." Because His Father has put "all things in subjection under His feet," we need never fear. In fact we can find joy in every intercessory battle in which He chooses to include us.[6]

REALISTIC ABOUT OUR ENEMY

In his classic book *The Screwtape Letters*, C. S. Lewis wrote, "There are two equal and opposite errors into which our race can fall about devils. One is to disbelieve in their existence. The other is to believe, and to feel an excessive and unhealthy interest in them. They themselves are equally pleased with both errors."[7]

There are vast numbers of believers who, due to an unhealthy spiritual naiveté, never embrace the warfare aspect

> Satan and his demons are a force to be reckoned with on a regular basis.

of the Christian journey. Oblivious to the hosts of evil that are out to destroy them, they treat Satan as a concept rather than a very real being. This was my own experience in my early Christian life. My circle of believing friends and family joked at times about his influence ("The devil made me do it"), but for all practical purposes just ignored him, not seeing Satan and his demons as a force to be reckoned with on a regular basis. Knowing what I now know about how he operates, I have no doubt that the evil one took great pleasure in my ignorance.

Of course, the other extreme is to glorify the demonic, to make Satan and his power out to be far greater than it is. Movies on exorcism and even some Christian books on deliverance reflect a perilous preoccupation with the occult, and they can leave people cowering in fear instead of standing in the authority of Jesus Christ, who promises to crush Satan under our feet (Romans 16:20). My desire for this chapter is that we will be able to dismiss both of these extremes as we develop a healthy understanding of what our enemy is like and how we are to engage in battle for the kingdom in an ongoing, practical way.

THE TERRITORY IN OUR OWN HEARTS

If I were to ask what things keep you from praying the way you'd like, what would you say? I spoke in the first chapter of how each of us has already been made an intercessor through the work of Christ—this is our call, our joy, and our crown. But, sadly, many of us never find the freedom to live up to our destiny. Always under a cloud of guilt, we make resolutions to do better but can't seem to get where we want to be in our prayer lives. Have you ever considered that we might be up against something greater than our lack of discipline or overcommitted schedules? That our inability to embrace our identity as intercessors is being thwarted by something beyond what the eye can see?

Consider, for example, the three disciples who went with Jesus into the garden the night He was arrested. His request that they stay and keep watch while He prayed was the only time He'd ever asked any of them for help. But in Christ's most desperate hour, what did His closest followers do? They went to sleep—something to which I can readily relate. That piercing question Jesus asked not once, but three different times—"Can you not pray for one hour?"— breeds conviction in my soul every time I read the story. But *why* couldn't the disciples stay awake and pray?

Is it possible that the hosts of hell played a part in this? Could it be that the weaknesses or sins in the hearts of these men had opened a door for Satan to dull their minds and bodies into a sleep that almost seemed drug-induced? I don't want to belabor this point, but we must at least consider the possibility that the difficulties those three faced in intercession, and the difficulties we come up against as well, may be the result of something more than the frailty of our flesh.

Satan's goal is to keep us from living out our call as intercessors, primarily because he knows it will lead to more of Jesus in us and through us and around us, something every force of darkness detests. If he can't keep us from having a desire to pray in the first place, which is one of his most effective strategies, Satan will work in dozens of ways to disrupt, discourage, and defeat us every time we do set out to intercede.

But the Prince of Darkness does not work in a vacuum. He is the god of this world, which means that he has already done everything he can to promote and exalt cultural values that directly violate those of Christ's kingdom. Arming himself with these things, he aims his fiery darts at our flesh. Always looking for places of vulnerability in our wounds and weaknesses and sin, Satan's demonic hosts stalk in stealth until they see an opening and then go for the kill, peppering us with lies and accusations and inflicting various degrees of oppression upon us.

What this means is that in order to engage in prayer for others as we really want to, we must address the areas of spiritual bondage in our own lives. Because there will always be issues of the heart that need to be wrested from Satan's influence and yielded to Christ, reclaiming that territory should be our first line of attack against him. Effectiveness in battling on behalf of others in prayer depends first and foremost on how diligently we fight this good fight at home, for, as in the infamous words of the comic strip character Pogo, "We have met the enemy and he is us."

UNDERSTANDING STRONGHOLDS

Paul addressed how we go about this in his second letter to the church at Corinth. He wrote, "Though we walk in the flesh, we do not war according to the flesh, for the weapons of our warfare are not of the flesh, but divinely powerful for the destruction of fortresses" (2 Corinthians 10:3–4). The key word here is *fortresses*, which can be translated as "stronghold." It comes from the root word *fortify*, which describes a secured dwelling, a physical place of protection from which one can wage war.[8]

Let me try to illustrate it this way. One of the battles our military engaged in was to secure the freedom of a city controlled by insurgents who had holed themselves up in a mosque. Due to the ramifications of attacking a holy shrine, our soldiers could do very little to combat the endless rounds of mortar fire coming their way. Because they were effectively barred from blowing up this enemy stronghold, victory could not be secured. From their place of protection, the insurgents were able to hold the entire city captive.

In the same way, Satan has fortified his position against the work of Christ within us on any number of issues. It is as if he has holed himself up in the sanctuary of our minds and, from that place, continually attacks and renders us ineffective. Because strongholds have usually developed over years of erroneous thinking and sinful behavior, we'll have to do more than make a decision to change if we want to tear them down.

Paul wrote, "We are destroying speculations and every lofty thing raised up against the knowledge of God, and we are taking every thought captive to the obedience of Christ" (2 Corinthians 10:5). The picture Paul painted is an aggressive one—we're going in through the power of God's Spirit and destroying the bunkers behind which Satan has hidden in order to keep up his assault on us. How do we do this? Though there is no universal formula, Scripture does provide some principles, which when applied can become mighty weapons of our warfare.[9] What I would like to do is share one of the fortresses I have had to confront in this area, laying out how I worked through it, so that you can apply these principles to your life.

Let's define a stronghold in intercession as any wrongful pattern of thinking or way of relating that Satan uses to keep us from praying for others, a privilege that every disciple of Christ is entitled to enjoy. Let me stress first that there is a key difference between weaknesses or occasional sins and a spiritual stronghold. A stronghold is something that is *always* working against us. For example, if you've confessed your failure to intercede over and over and still are not finding victory, or if you have tried to discipline yourself to pray but never feel that you're getting anywhere, then it may be time to deal with a stronghold where Satan is at work. Here are the four components we will look at:

1. Identification: pinpointing the stronghold and the lies behind it
2. Confession: agreeing with God about the sin(s) the stronghold reflects

3. Renunciation: firmly rejecting the influence Satan has had through the stronghold

4. Repentance: walking in the opposite direction of the stronghold

Identification

Identification is the most important thing we'll do, and often the most difficult. To pinpoint a stronghold or the lies that have contributed to it requires God to open our eyes to something we have simply been unable to recognize on our own. We may need the guidance and prayer of other believers to work through this point, but coming to terms with what is really going on must be our first step in the dismantling process.

In the example I'm going to share, I had noticed over a period of time that when I prayed for someone, random thoughts would come to mind, such as *This won't make any difference* or *You know you don't really believe this can help* or *Why are you wasting your time anyway?* I tried to ignore this and keep praying, but it was a great struggle. Before long, without even realizing it, I was rarely asking God for anything, and when I did, my requests were halfhearted or duty-driven. One day, while in a time of prayer with others, the Lord impressed on someone's heart that I was struggling with a stronghold of *unbelief,* and I knew immediately they were right. But where had it come from, and why did it have such a hold on me now?

Before I answer that, let me say that I suspect *unbelief* is a stronghold common to many of us, and for good reason.

I suspect *unbelief* is a stronghold common to many of us, and for good reason.

The dictionary defines the word *unbelief* as "withholding of belief; doubt; incredulity; skepticism,"[10] and it is easy to see how Satan uses the values of our culture to attack us in this area. We live in a skeptical society when it comes to matters of faith. The demonic world-view of humanism has made a god of the human mind, causing us to form our values based on what we can see and touch and feel and measure. There is a growing scorn in every arena—from education to government to entertainment—toward those who base their lives and decisions upon a spiritual reality beyond what the eye can see.

As Christians, we may not realize the ways in which our culture has shaped how we view the things God says in His Word, especially in regard to prayer and the heavenly realm. But if we look hard at how we live, we will see the ways unbelief manifests itself. For example, there was a time when I avoided enlisting people to pray for me as I ministered in writing or speaking. I would tell myself that I didn't want to be a bother, but in reality I was embracing self-reliance and not believing that apart from Christ I could do nothing.

Not only are fortresses of unbelief constructed with stones comprising harmful cultural values, but our own experiences and weaknesses play a part as well. When something we've long prayed for doesn't happen, stones of niggling doubt or discouragement may find a place in our hearts. When we've asked and received an answer completely different from what we expected, stones of resentment or disappointment can wedge their way in. When we've tried to intercede consistently but know of people who seem to get far greater results, stones of insecurity or self-protection may find an easy fit. Before we know it, the evil one has a secure dwelling place in our minds, from which he can easily keep us from winning the battle against prayerlessness.

For me, the stronghold of unbelief had been formed over time as a result of unanswered prayer. For years I had cried out for revival, specifically in our church and community. Principles in Scripture and promises that I felt the Spirit had given me sustained a journey of intercession for revival through many ups and downs. But then some severe trials our church was going through began to shake my confidence, and I slowly lost that sense of passionate desire. (I'll share more about that in the next chapter.) I had no idea my walk with God, and particularly my joy in praying for others, was being sabotaged.

When God revealed the stronghold of unbelief, I saw that underneath it were things like self-protection and fear. Because I didn't want to feel the hurt of being disappointed with God anymore and was afraid to confront the hard questions of why He hadn't fulfilled His promises, I simply stopped asking. In probing deeper I recognized a plethora of lies that were subtly insinuating themselves into my spiritual life—that God wasn't wise, that His plans were not perfect, that He didn't really speak, that His Word could not be trusted, and on and on. Though I would have rejected any such notions on a conscious level, my failure to intercede told a different story. Seeing this was the first critical step in tearing down a stronghold that had a far greater impact on me than I ever would have guessed.

Confession

Once we have identified the stronghold and the lies behind it, we need to agree with God about the sin involved. To confess means to stop covering up or excusing and instead directly confront the sins of our hearts and our actions. In my situation, I had to admit both my lack of prayer and all the ways in which I had doubted God's Word and His character. But that wasn't all. The Spirit then opened my eyes to other sins such as pride, hypocrisy, deceit, legalism, and self-reliance, all of which were related to my unbelief.

Confession is critical because we aren't trying to make minor changes, like renovating one room in a house, but instead want to bring a wrecking ball to bear on the entire fortress. When we fail to deal with all the things God wants to reveal, we may leave cracks through which Satan can reinstate his warring position in our minds.

Although there may be brokenness and tears of godly sorrow at this point, this is not meant to be an exercise in morbid introspection. We do not need to labor over every smidgen of possibly sinful behavior, beating ourselves up as we go, but rather we need to simply trust the God of the universe, who alone can reveal what is at the heart of our struggle. Our call is simply to walk through the process in intimacy with Christ and rest in the reality that when the

Holy Spirit convicts and we confess, He forgives and cleanses us of all unrighteousness—conscious or otherwise—concerning this stronghold.

Renunciation

The third step—renouncing Satan's influence through the stronghold—is one of the most powerful tools we have in our arsenal against him, but it is so simple we often fail to use it. James tells us to "resist the devil and he will flee" (James 4:7). To resist means to set ourselves in opposition, not only against Satan, but against his army of demons as well—those supernatural beings the Bible calls the rulers, powers, world forces of this darkness, and spiritual forces of wickedness in the heavenly places (Ephesians 6:12).

This is where some of us can begin to feel a bit uncomfortable. We don't have any problem agreeing with God about our sins, but to go beyond that and bind the dark forces that have energized them is another story. Yet if we don't take this step, we will probably never walk in the full freedom God intends. For example, after I'd identified the stronghold of unbelief in my life and confessed the sins involved, I began to experience some measure of freedom in intercession once again. But there were times I found myself assaulted by skeptical thoughts about prayer. These seemed to come out of left field and were often quite bizarre, such as scorning the idea of God's existence or challenging the authenticity of my relationship with Him. The thoughts did not stop until I took spiritual authority over their source.

When we read of the temptations of Jesus, there seems

to be a twofold process in resisting the devil. First, we speak God's Word aloud—no sermons needed, just the short and simple truth—as Jesus did. For example, I might say something like this:

Satan, you are a liar when you try to make me doubt God's Word or His character. God does hear my prayers and answer. He is perfect in all His ways. His Word says that nothing is impossible with Him, that He hears the cries of His elect and answers speedily, and that He will accomplish His purposes concerning me.

The second part of the process is to stand against Satan directly as Jesus did when He said, "Get out of here, Satan" (Matthew 4:10 NLT). Behind our words is the conviction that in Jesus's name we want nothing else to do with Satan or his forces, that we are closing the door of sin through which they once had access, and therefore they must go. When done as a part of this process, resisting the devil can bring powerful and immediate results. I am amazed at how those random thoughts have lost their power over me—not that Satan hasn't tried to blindside me with lies, but because the back of unbelief has been broken, I am able to recognize and renounce the thoughts when they come.

Repentance

Repentance is that which produces the greatest change and can bring joy back into the areas over which Satan has had victory. In the New Testament, to repent means to radically change not only one's thinking, but also one's actions in the given area—to make a turnabout midstream. The practical application in intercession is to ask God what the opposite attitude and behavior would be from the stronghold we've been bound by, and then seek by His grace to walk in it.

This can involve any number of things. For example, if your view of God has been damaged, then spending time reacquainting yourself with His character and ways and developing a fresh intimacy with Him might be a good place to start. If you've hidden your lack of prayer from others or often broken promises to pray, then sharing openly and transparently of your sin as you ask for help in moving toward greater authenticity would be a possibility. The goal is to let God's Spirit enable you to begin walking down the road to complete restoration and away from the destruction Satan has wrought through the stronghold in your life.

In my case, repentance was pretty straightforward. First, I needed to spend some time renewing my mind with the truth of God's Word concerning prayer. Then I needed to be intentional about intercession once again. For example, when someone asked me to pray for them, I would do so right then, affirming by my action that I believed God can and does answer prayer. I also began to practice random intercession— lifting up the concerns of others whenever someone came to mind, reminding myself that

Resisting the devil can bring powerful and immediate results.

prayer makes a difference, whether I get to see the results or not. A major means of repentance for me was to replace a lot of giving advice or problem solving with lifting others up in prayer. And finally, I made the choice to begin to cry out for revival once again, determined—this time by God's grace—to cling to His promises until the day I die, if need be. This kind of repentance can be an exciting challenge as it restores in us the true joy of our salvation.

When we employ these four simple weapons, the results will be almost tangible—as if a great weight has been lifted from our shoulders. This is a time to rejoice, to give thanks, and to receive a new measure of fullness from the Spirit of God, who now delights to make Himself at home in the place the evil one had secured in our minds. Though unbelief is a significant stronghold for intercessors, there will certainly be others we need to deal with along the way. Dismantling Satan's fortresses can become a way of life, a very normal part of God's work as He sanctifies us completely—body, soul, and spirit. As He does so, we will experience more and more in a practical way that the weapons of our warfare are indeed powerful ones.

OUR HIGH CALLING

The highest gain in this process is that it frees us to do the greater works Jesus has called us to do through engaging in spiritual warfare on behalf of others. I don't think there is a more beautiful description of what this can mean than in the

passage Jesus chose in His first public address at the syna-
gogue in His hometown. Reading the words of the prophet
Isaiah, He said:

> The Spirit of the Lord is upon Me, because He anointed
> Me to preach the gospel to the poor. He has sent Me to
> proclaim release to the captives, and recovery of sight to
> the blind, to set free those who are oppressed, to proclaim
> the favorable year of the Lord. (Luke 4:18–19)

"As the Father has sent me, I also send you," Jesus proclaimed in John 20:21, but have we embraced this high calling? Do we really believe we can be a part of something so
profound as to see people walk—freedom papers in hand—
through the gates of sin that have held them in bondage? To
somehow play a role, however small, in opening the eyes of
the blind to the light of God's glory? Are we aware as we
drive down the street or sit in the pew at church that we have
the privilege of co-laboring with Christ to lift the oppression
from the broken, hurting people that surround us? Can we
comprehend at all that this is the age of grace, that out of the
entire human race throughout all of history, we are the ones
who have been chosen to usher in the year of the Lord's favor
to a world so desperate for His healing touch?

When we think of that with which God has entrusted
us, something powerful ought to rise up within. A righteous
wrath should fill our hearts as we watch the destruction the
evil one has wrought in the lives of people created to bring
honor and glory to God. That demonic entities seem to have

free rein in a world belonging to our holy King is an outrage that we simply cannot ignore. As Richard Foster so powerfully noted:

> Behind absentee landlords of ghetto apartments are the spiritual forces of greed and avarice. In back of unreasoned and excessive resistance to the Gospel message are demonic forces of disobedience and distraction. Underneath the organized structures of injustice and oppression are principalities of privilege and status. Aiding and abetting the sexual violence and the race hate and the child molestation that are such a part of modern society are diabolical powers of destruction and brutality.[11]

God once made this startling announcement: "I have commanded My consecrated ones, I have even called My mighty warriors, My proudly exulting ones, to execute My anger" (Isaiah 13:3). The Almighty is full of wrath against Satan and his hosts, who ever live to rob, steal, kill, and destroy. Though God has determined every demon's destiny to be eternal destruction in the lake of fire, today He commands us to go into battle, to execute His fury against their work. Every time we watch the spoiler chalk up another victory, a war cry should erupt from our innermost being. In commissioning you and me to be His mighty warriors, our Lord makes us capable of the fiercest fight on His behalf.

I remember the first time the sense of this commissioning welled up within me. I'd received a phone call that a relative who had committed his life to Christ after years of drug and alcohol addiction had suffered a relapse. After having prayed so long for his salvation and having seen his zeal for the Lord grow by leaps and bounds, I was incensed by this news and immediately went to prayer. Envisioning the host of demonic activity that Jesus warned would take place when demons returned to a house swept clean, I found myself marching around doing battle, my voice getting louder and louder. Soon I was yelling and stomping—conduct I can assure you was completely out of character for me—and binding and loosing until an hour had passed and I fell into a chair, exhausted.

Here's the thing: I don't think for a minute that my frenetic activity was evidence of great faith or amazing power in prayer. I was just furious and didn't really know any other way to express the fire in my gut. I believe this is what was really happening: I was simply executing God's own anger, something I want to learn to do more and more.

Beyond the Need at Hand

Spiritual warfare can never be reduced to steps or formulas, for our enemy is a clever foe. Three different times in his letters to the churches, Paul warned us to be aware of Satan's *schemes*, a word that denotes craftiness, cunning, wiliness, and trickery.[12] It is critical when we battle in prayer for another that we take the time to seek the Lord and listen to His voice, asking for insight into the strategies Satan has implemented. This becomes our warfare agenda,

> Though we do not wrestle against flesh and blood, we must indeed wrestle, for we have a vicious enemy who lurks in the shadows and works in the dark of night.

rather than the need at hand. For example, someone who struggles with Internet pornography may be bound by a stronghold of rejection based on childhood experiences and the lies that ensued. Someone who suffers from depression may be under the influence of a stronghold of anger from some unresolved conflict or lack of forgiveness. Often, even physical ailments can have their root in territory of the soul to which Satan is always seeking to stake a claim.

This can be an enlightening process for parents as we plead on behalf of our children. If our teenagers rebel, we can recognize that there may be forces of darkness stoking the fires of resentment that so easily flare up as the result of adolescent hormones. When a young child withdraws from social contact or begins to walk in fear, we may realize that there are demonic beings pouncing upon their weaknesses or wounds with lies they can't possibly confront. We are their spiritual protectors, and through intercession we can take authority over these works of Satan in our children's lives.

Above all we must remember that though we do not wrestle against flesh and blood, we must indeed wrestle, for we have a vicious enemy who lurks in the shadows and works in the dark of night. We must go forward with confidence, knowing that Jesus, in whom all authority in heaven and on earth rests, has paved the way. In His name we withstand the forces of darkness as we unleash God's power to destroy the works of the enemy in hearts and lives and communities and nations of the world.

STAY THE COURSE

When we take up our call as warfare intercessors, we soon learn that victory is rarely quick. There may be occasions when we see God move at once, but it is more likely that the situations we face will require us to engage in battle after battle, for this is the nature of war. In a rare glimpse into the combat arena known as the heavenly places, Scripture tells the story of how some demons over Persia held back a messenger of God from bringing Daniel the answer to his prayers for a period of twenty-one days (Daniel 10). The point is simply this: Because we do not know what is taking place in the unseen world, we must persevere in prayer for others as long as God continues to burden our hearts and give us grace to intercede. The victory isn't complete until every effort of the enemy is thwarted, and only God knows when that will be.

I experienced this firsthand a couple of years ago. My husband was working in the yard when he began to feel feverish and was overtaken by a deep cough. Though he was never really sick, the cough plagued him for weeks, growing worse until the pain in his rib cage was unbearable and sleep impossible. One day some friends who were praying for us sensed God saying that the enemy was afflicting my husband and we needed to battle in prayer for him. Together, the four of us first asked God to reveal any access points Satan might have had in Joe's heart. After Joe prayed through a few things, we all joined in spiritual warfare against the evil one and any powers of darkness that might have been involved.

When we were finished, we fully expected the cough to go away. But it didn't—at least not right off. In fact, he seemed to get worse over the next few weeks. Since the doctors had given it their best shot, all we could do was keep battling in prayer. Then one day, for no apparent reason, Joe felt an unusual peace and decided to take a nap, something he'd been unable to do for a few months. He quickly fell into a deep sleep, and as he awoke, he heard the words *it's over*. Feeling a warm, tingling breeze blow across his body, he knew that the cough was gone.

God had performed a miracle, but for months I secretly questioned whether Joe's sickness could really have been the work of spiritual entities (though Scripture makes it clear that Jesus healed many physical illnesses brought on by Satan). Then one night something happened that sealed it for me once and for all. Joe and I were getting ready to pray for a group of our church members who were ministering overseas, when he was struck with chills and that infamous cough returned out of nowhere. I grabbed a blanket and went to get the thermometer and some aspirin, when it dawned on me that this might be Satan's doing. When I returned, Joe was shaking almost uncontrollably, so we joined together in prayer, commanding every force of darkness to flee in the name of Jesus. Within minutes the symptoms completely disappeared, and we were able to spend the time in intercession as we'd originally set out to do.

I cannot tell you why God waited to heal Joe the very first time or why He allowed Satan to afflict him again. I think it has something to do with the things our Father wants to teach us about intercession—that seeing results isn't about our prayers but His power, that the struggles with Satan's forces are real and tangible, and that taking authority means holding on in faith over time. God is truly training our hands for war and, to that end, does not always bring quick resolution to the struggles we face. Our course is to stand as warriors through every skirmish until we see the victory secured.

KEEPING SIGHT OF THE BIG PICTURE

These kinds of delays in spiritual warfare can be exciting if we maintain our vision of the big picture. God's goal is to radiate the wonder of His glory by transforming us into His image, which can take place only as we walk in continual intimacy with Him. The battles we face in intercession are a small slice of a grand scheme, one in which ultimately, as someone once said, Satan is God's errand boy. Every time we face a situation where prayer is needed to defeat the enemy's schemes against us or someone else, God is accomplishing His purposes to keep us close to Him, dependent upon Him, and ever learning of His amazing ways.

He demonstrated this with the Israelites in their early

Jesus is the Truth that girds us and the Righteousness that protects our hearts.

years in the Promised Land. When Joshua died, not all of Israel's enemies had been driven out, something Scripture indicates God planned ahead of time. Why? Because He knew that a generation would be raised up who had not seen His mighty power and therefore would have to experience war for themselves to understand their need of Him. With every assault of an enemy, God had the opportunity to test their hearts and see if they had come to the place where they knew He was their only hope (Judges 2–3).

The work God is doing in each of us through spiritual warfare often transcends the answers we are looking for as intercessors. He ever seeks to draw us to Himself, to test our hearts and prove to us that He is a God who rides the heavens to our help, who comes to us in His majesty. He is our eternal dwelling place; He shelters us with everlasting arms and thrusts out our enemies before us as He commands their destruction (Deuteronomy 33:26–27). This must be the vision that captivates and keeps us on course as we battle daily for the glory of His name.

RETURN TO OUR REST

I want to share one last thing that is critical as we engage in warfare intercession, which is that our power and joy in it depend on learning to rest in Christ's finished work. In his classic book on Ephesians, Watchman Nee showed how Adam and Eve were created on the sixth day, and on the seventh—before doing anything else—they were called to rest, a progression our spiritual life should reflect as well. Yes, we are to stand against Satan, but as Nee pointed out, before we can walk or stand, we must learn how to make ourselves at home where we are seated with Christ in heavenly places. Nee wrote:

> What does it really mean to sit down? . . . In walking or standing we expend a great deal of energy, but when we are seated we relax at once, because the strain no longer falls upon our muscles and nerves but on something outside of ourselves. So also in the spiritual realm, to sit down is simply to rest our whole weight—our load, ourselves, our future, everything—upon the Lord. We let Him bear the responsibility and cease to carry it ourselves.[13]

This perspective transforms the way we view ourselves in spiritual warfare. When we get it, we'll do what David did—throw off every piece of ill-fitting armor and confidently go forth "in the name of the LORD of hosts" (1 Samuel 17:45). We will know that we are battle-ready only because of who we are in Christ, for it is His very essence that comprises the weapons of our warfare.

Jesus is the Truth that girds us and the Righteousness that protects our hearts. He is the Peace that prepares us for what is to come. He is our Shield and the One who infuses us with faith to deflect every one of Satan's fiery darts.

Having redeemed us by His blood, He sets our salvation upon our heads like a helmet, transforming our minds and keeping them from serious injury. Above all, Christ is the living Word, and as we abide in Him, we will be able to wield supernatural power like a sword to destroy the forces of wickedness coming against us and those for whom we pray (Ephesians 6:10–19).

Spiritual warfare is a wonder beyond our grasp. It is one more way God enables us to know His heart, to grow in intimate knowledge of His ways and be used by Him for glorious purposes. I think if we really understood what He has called and enabled us to do, we'd walk around awestruck, gratitude welling up in us for each opportunity we have to battle on behalf of another in prayer.

PRACTICING PRAYER

Once again we will pause to meditate on the prayers of other saints. Here's a format you can follow, but feel free to establish your own:

- Read these prayers silently through once, pondering the heart and meaning in them.
- Read each one aloud, as if it were your own.
- Journal your thoughts about what you have read, then write your own prayer.
- Read your written prayer to the Lord aloud.

A Prayer of Asaph for Victory Over His Enemies

(Psalm 83 nlt)

O God, don't sit idly by,
　　silent and inactive!
Don't you hear the tumult of your enemies?
　　Don't you see what your arrogant enemies are doing?
They devise crafty schemes against your people,
　　laying plans against your precious ones.
"Come," they say, "let us wipe out Israel as a nation.
　　We will destroy the very memory of its existence."
　　This was their unanimous decision.
They signed a treaty as allies against you—
　　these Edomites and Ishmaelites,
　　Moabites and Hagrites,
　　Gebalites, Ammonites, and Amalekites,
　　and people from Philistia and Tyre.
Assyria has joined them, too,
　　and is allied with the descendants of Lot. *Interlude*

Do to them as you did to the Midianites
　　or as you did to Sisera and Jabin at the Kishon River.
They were destroyed at Endor,
　　and their decaying corpses fertilized the soil.
Let their mighty nobles die as Oreb and Zeeb did.
　　Let all their princes die like Zebah and Zalmunna,

for they said, "Let us seize for our own use
    these pasturelands of God!"

O my God, blow them away like whirling dust,
    like chaff before the wind!
As a fire roars through a forest
    and as a flame sets mountains ablaze,
chase them with your fierce storms;
    terrify them with your tempests.
Utterly disgrace them
    until they submit to your name, O LORD.
Let them be ashamed and terrified forever.
    Make them failures in everything they do,
until they learn that you alone are called the LORD,
    that you alone are the Most High, supreme over all the
    earth.

A Prayer of Charles Wesley

Charles Wesley, born in the early eighteenth century, was known as the poet of the Methodist movement. He was an itinerant preacher for a short while in America but spent most of his life ministering in England. Though he shrank from human praise and disliked power and prominence, he was used mightily by God. In his lifetime, he wrote more

*than sixty-five hundred poems and hymns, many of which
are well-loved to this day.*

Arm of the Lord, awake, awake!
Thine own immortal strength put on!
With terror clothed, hell's kingdom shake,
And cast Thy foes with fury down!

As in the ancient days appear!
The sacred annals speak Thy fame:
Be now omnipotently near,
To endless ages still the same.

Thy arm, Lord, is not shortened now,
It wants not now the power to save;
Still present with Thy people, Thou
Bear'st them through life's disparted wave.

By death and hell pursued in vain
To Thee the ransomed seed shall come,
Shouting their heavenly Zion gain
And pass through death triumphant home.

The pain of life shall there be o'er,
The anguish and distracting care,
There sighing grief shall weep no more,
And sin shall never enter there.

Where pure, essential joy is found,
The Lord's redeemed their heads shall raise,
With everlasting gladness crowned,
And filled with love, and lost in praise.

LOOKING AHEAD

There is a kind of battle we face as believers that is different from our warfare against the forces of darkness—the wrestling we do with God Himself. Though He is always working things together for our good, the situations in which we find ourselves when we set out to intercede can make us feel as if God is fighting against us, and He is surely a formidable foe. This is when the questions come. Does God really hear and answer prayer? Why doesn't He answer mine? Do I lack faith? Does it really matter if I pray? Why does it take so long, and how am I supposed to keep trusting when it feels as if it really doesn't make a difference?

In the next chapter we will look at these things as we seek to understand the nature of faith and its relationship to God's sovereign purposes. I face these issues with a bit of fear and trepidation, feeling a need to warn you that my list of unanswered prayers seems a lot longer than those for which He has granted my requests. But the process has been a worthy one, and my delight in Jesus has only grown stronger along the way. In the end, isn't that what we're all really after?

CHAPTER SIX

LEARNING THE LANGUAGE OF FAITH

*Praying until the Answers
Come . . . and What
to Do When They Don't*

*Lose the importunity of prayer . . . lose
the real conflict of will and will, lose the
habit of wrestling and the hope of prevailing with God, make it mere walking
with God in friendly talk; and precious
as that is, yet you tend to lose the reality
of prayer at last.*

P. T. FORSYTH[1]

Sometimes God invites us on a journey that if we knew from the start where it would take us, we might politely decline to go along. But the Almighty—wise and winsome and well aware of our weaknesses—moves in quietly, wooing us like a suitor until we find ourselves bearing a burden bigger than our faith and carrying it longer than we planned, if we planned at all. When this happens, it is a rare gift, one that we will never be the same for having opened. I know because I've talked to many prayer warriors along the way who, except for a few details, tell the same tale. I know because it happened to me, and almost everything I've learned about faith came through that experience. This is the story I must tell.

On March 23, 1993, the Lord began to speak to my heart about a work He was going to do in our community and the church my husband and I had planted eleven years prior. At the time, I knew very little about hearing God's voice, but in the quiet of my devotions, I sensed a stream of words in my spirit and knew I needed to write them down. Following is an excerpt from my writings on that day:

I have a work to do in the very heart of New Hope. Do not look to the left or to the right but only to Me. I will make the path straight, but it will lead through many days of darkness . . . In the midst of the darkest days My Light will begin to shine, and it will increase to a vast flame that will bring to life those frozen by woundedness, weakness, and sin. And I will rejoice over you to do you good, and I will faithfully plant you in the land with all My heart and with all My soul.

Not having any idea what I ought to do with this, I decided not to tell anyone and just wait and see what might happen.

The pilgrimage that followed was one of great hope and joyful yearnings, yet it was fraught with frustration and failure as well. I was often tempted to let God and myself off the hook by explaining those words away as some kind of vain imagination, but He kept pursuing me, a reality for which I am deeply grateful. Because if He hadn't, I would not have learned the awesome joy of wrestling with Him, of crying out, as Jacob did, that I wasn't going to let go until He blessed me. I would not have experienced the exquisite mystery of prayer without words, of groanings so deep there is no language to adequately express them.

I would not have discovered that faith is far more profound than some kind of currency with which we buy answers to prayer. I would not have learned about obtaining a testimony and why God's responses often look like the scorpions and snakes Jesus said a good father would never give. Most of all, I would not have experienced the wonder of a Lord who rewards those who seek Him with gifts far greater than the ones they'd sought.

WHAT I DON'T KNOW

I'll share that story and its unsettling stages later, but first I want to offer some biblical principles concerning faith. For many years I have been disturbed by the amount of dogma in the Christian community concerning the issue of faith, which leaves people with little confidence and a lot of guilt about prayer. I hope to show that faith is a gift God grants to each of us, and faith can be a very simple thing, once we understand what the Bible says about it. At the same time, there are some questions concerning faith that I cannot answer and some issues that perplex me still as an intercessor. Since it seems only fair that you know what these are from the start, this is where I'll begin.

First of all, I do not know why God answers some prayers and doesn't answer others. It's not that there isn't a list of good reasons—our sin, His will, impure motives, the greater plan, etc. But there are times when these aren't enough to settle my soul,

Faith is far more profound than some kind of currency with which we buy answers to prayer.

when I can't come up with a logical explanation for God's failure to do the things I've asked on behalf of others.

I shared in an earlier chapter of the joy in being used to pray for the release of Heather Mercer and Dayna Curry, hostages in Afghanistan. Shortly after I saw success in that prayer venture, terrorists in the Philippines abducted a missionary couple by the name of Martin and Gracia Burnham. For the next year they were held captive and deprived of even the most basic human rights while our government worked to bring a peaceful end to the crisis.

Since the prayer chain for Heather and Dayna was already in place, it was easy for me to enlist my group to intercede for the Burnhams. In both cases, thousands of people from all over the world were praying, and churches held twenty-four-hour prayer vigils that lasted the duration of their captivity. But with the Burnhams, the outcome was very different. They were held not weeks, but months, and only Gracia survived, being rescued while clinging to her dead husband, who was most likely a victim of friendly fire by a confused SWAT team.

I struggle with this—not because I think God made some kind of mistake, but because I wonder what role prayer played in either situation. If seeing God's answer depends on the number of people praying or the intensity of their prayers, then the Burnhams ought to have enjoyed the same kind of triumphant end that Heather and Dayna did. This situation, along with many others I have faced in my intercessory life, is why I must say that I simply do not know what causes God to answer some prayers and not others.

Another thing I do not know is how to reconcile the sovereignty of God and the will of the human soul. Scripture is abundantly clear that God has complete foreknowledge and full control of this universe and its inhabitants. David wrote, "Even before there is a word on my tongue, behold, O LORD, You know it all"; and another psalmist proclaimed, "Our God is in the heavens; He does whatever He pleases" (Psalms 139:4; 115:3). King Nebuchadnezzar, after being disciplined for his pride, declared this about Jehovah: "He does according to His will in the host of heaven and among the inhabitants of earth; and no one can ward off His hand or say to Him, 'What have You done?'" (Daniel 4:35).

Indeed, God is sovereign, but at the same time Scripture teaches that He offers us the opportunity to be involved, through intercession, in shaping the very future that He already knows. There are even stories that seem to imply we have the power to change God's mind. For example, when the Israelites built the golden calf, God told Moses to leave Him alone so His anger could burn against them. When Moses interceded, however, Scripture says, "The LORD changed His mind about the harm which He said He would do to His people" (Exodus 32:14). In another case, God told Hezekiah that he was going to die. Hezekiah wept and prayed, and the Scripture says God instructed the prophet Isaiah, "Go and say to Hezekiah, 'Thus says the LORD, the God of your father David, "I have heard your prayer, I have seen your tears; behold, I will add fifteen years to your life"'" (Isaiah 38:5).

So how do we square these seemingly irreconcilable

truths—that God is sovereign and that we have the capacity to influence His decisions and actions on this earth? I have heard and read many explanations on both sides of the issue, but I won't take the time to offer them here because, to be honest, none of them completely resolve it for me. I am willing to live with the dissonance in these two truths, and I trust God to settle it for me when and if He so chooses. His ways and thoughts are infinitely above mine, and in this I rest.

Finally, I do not know how much faith is enough to get the job done. I remember my car breaking down in a rainstorm once when my first son was a toddler. Not having a great deal of faith at that moment, I asked my son to pray that God would help us. He acquiesced with all the confident aplomb of a two-year-old, and as soon as he finished, I turned the key and the car started. I'll never forget his childlike glee as he said, "It works, Mom—it really works!"

I wish prayer were always that simple, but for me, some of the things I've believed God for the most and cried out for the longest remain unanswered for no apparent reason. I think that I've learned a lot about what faith looks like and how it pleases God, but at the same time I cannot say there is some sort of clear and consistent pattern in my life that connects my level of faith to the degree of answered prayer. I have to say right off that I do not know how much faith is enough.

FINDING FAITH

What is *faith*? How do we know if we've got it? When the New Testament uses this word, it usually speaks of strong persuasion, trust, and confidence. The author of Hebrews wrote that faith is "the assurance of things hoped for, the conviction of things not seen" (Hebrews 11:1). In other words, we know that we have faith when we are experiencing an inner assurance and the conviction that not only is God able to answer our prayers, but He will.

But then what are we to do when this inner assurance is lacking? How do we pray for someone when there is no conviction in our hearts that God is going to answer our prayers? This is an important question, especially since Scripture teaches that faith can move God to action, and a lack of faith may keep us from receiving from Him.[2] The solution is simpler than we realize: We go to the source. Faith for intercession is no different from saving faith—both are a gift from God, "not as a result of works, so that no one may boast" (Ephesians 2:9). Paul confirmed this when he noted that God has allotted to each of us a measure of faith (Romans 12:3).

This explains to some degree why Jesus was always chiding His disciples about their lack of faith. Take, for example, Peter's water-walking debut, where he fell after a few steps. Jesus rebuked him, saying, "O you of little faith."

I think we'd all have to agree that Peter's getting out of that boat and walking on water was no small feat, so what was Jesus's point? Why would He say this, given His claim that faith as small as a mustard seed could move a mountain? I believe that

I do not know how much faith is enough to get the job done.

what He was trying to establish was that because faith is something that comes from God, if we lack it, we need only fix our eyes upon Him, something Peter had failed to do.

Scripture says that faith comes from hearing, and hearing through the word of Christ (Romans 10:17). The language here speaks of that personal, intimate word we hear in our hearts when we listen to the voice of Jesus. In those times when we find we don't have assurance for the burdens God is giving us in prayer, we have only one recourse—to run back to the author and finisher of our faith and ask Him to help us in our unbelief (Hebrews 12:2; Mark 9:24). As Hallesby encourages us:

> I need not exert myself and try to force myself to believe, or try to chase doubt out of my heart. Both are equally useless. It begins to dawn on me that I can bring everything to Jesus, no matter how difficult it is, and I need not be frightened away by my doubts or my weak faith, but only tell Jesus how weak my faith is.[3]

When we bring our doubts and weaknesses to God and He gives us the faith we've been lacking, we can rejoice, for now we have the *assurance* that He will give us what we've hoped for. But there will also be times when God doesn't impart faith, even when we've cried out for it. Why? It may be that we are trying to carry a burden God does not intend for us at the time. He once told Jeremiah, as he pleaded for Israel, that he should stop praying for their welfare, that even if Moses and Samuel were to stand before Him, He would not hear (Jeremiah 14:11; 15:1). In this case it was because of their rebellion, but there may be other reasons in God's sovereign wisdom that He does not plan to heed our intercessions at the time we are asking, and thus does not provide us with the faith to press ahead in prayer.

It seems to me that when we have asked for faith and still don't have an inner conviction that God is going to answer, we have a couple of options. One is to keep asking, as Jeremiah did, trusting that we will receive the faith we need in God's time, if we are indeed praying that which is according to His will. On the other hand, we may need to set that particular request aside until God makes our role in the situation or His plan for it clear.

STRENGTHENING OUR FAITH

Though we cannot conjure up faith, we can strengthen that which we already have. Faith is like a muscle—the more we use it, the stronger it becomes. Because God knows this, at times He may offer us the opportunity to exercise our faith by setting up conditions for us to meet in order for Him to answer our prayers. This can feel a little risky because it may require us to take a stand that others won't understand. Yet like the lepers who had to head for the temple to be declared clean before they saw their healing, we, too, may be asked to act in confident assurance long before we see the answers in front of us.

I remember my first experience with this as a young

woman. I had been praying for my older sister Carol since the time I was twelve years old when my father shared with our family that she wouldn't be living at home anymore due to her lifestyle choices. After almost a decade of rebellion, Carol surprised us all when she showed up the week of my wedding. Pale and thin and with a boyfriend and a statue of Buddha in tow, which they promptly placed in our backyard for their yoga exercises (to which my father promptly took an ax the next morning), my dreams of her salvation were crushed.

Amid the joyful atmosphere of wedding celebrations, I was deeply grieved and shared my angst with a dear old saint. She talked with me of faith and asked what it would look like if God did answer my prayers for Carol. Then she suggested that since I'd been asking for so long, perhaps it was time to let God know I really believed He was going to answer. As we interceded together, I sensed a new confidence and peace and couldn't wait to see what would happen.

That night I told my parents and some other godly relatives that I felt God was leading me to stop asking and simply start believing. I laid out all the things I expected God to do in Carol's life and encouraged them to do the same. From that point forward, I simply thanked God for a sister who loved Jesus, who served Him faithfully and rejected all the trappings of Eastern religion that had held her in bondage for so many years. Though things seemed to get worse at first, I continued to thank God for the miracle to come. Two weeks later, Carol had a dramatic conversion experience and has served Jesus faithfully ever since.

When God leads us to act upon the faith He is giving us in prayer, it is important that we don't misunderstand His purpose. Demonstrating faith is not like some kind of magic formula that forces God to respond by earning us the right to get our prayers answered.[4] Instead, by taking action in obedience to His leading, we are exercising our faith muscles so that they can grow stronger for our next prayer venture. Over the course of a lifetime, we will develop an ability to endure in faith until we receive the thing that God has promised, through even the most daunting obstacles (Hebrews 10:36).

How God Sees Faith

The Bible tells us that anything not of faith is sin, and that without faith it is impossible to please God, but what does this mean (Romans 14:23; Hebrews 11:6)? Are we in sin if we harbor doubts? Does He turn His back in displeasure if we face uncertainty or encounter struggles when we're trying to lift others up? Surely not. Consider Abraham—the *father* of faith—who Scripture says did not waver in unbelief (Romans 4:20). This is a strange statement, given the fact that shortly after receiving the promise of an heir, Abraham grew tired of waiting on God and took things into his own hands to sire a son through Sarah's handmaiden. The answer lies in the word *waver*, which in

Demonstrating faith is not like some kind of magic formula that forces God to respond by earning us the right to get our prayers answered.

> The kind of faith that perseveres, feeble though it may be at times, is what brings pleasure to our Lord's heart.

this case means "to not pronounce judgment or form an opinion on account of."[5]

In other words, though Abraham must have often looked at his situation and questioned whether God was going to come through, over the course of his life he did not form an opinion against God and His promises. In fact, the mistakes he made and the struggles he endured served only to enable Abraham to grow stronger in faith and give God glory. The kind of faith that perseveres, feeble though it may be at times, is what brings pleasure to our Lord's heart.

This truth is at the heart of the story of the importunate widow, although we often miss the point. Jesus sets up the crux of what He wants to say by contrasting Himself to an egocentric judge who finally gives in to the widow's request just to get her off his back. He seems to be saying that if a lout like that would respond to a needy soul's persistent pleading, then it is preposterous to think that God won't answer when His very own people cry out to Him. But then Jesus adds the zinger: "However, when the Son of Man comes, will He find faith on the earth?" (Luke 18:8).

What God wants us to know here is that there is never a question of whether He hears our cries, but what matters to Him is our willingness to keep coming back, regardless of how impossible the situation seems or how long He delays in answering. We need to know this, because as intercessors we're so prone to focus on everything else—how long we pray, how intensely we pray, how zealous we feel, and so on. But God is looking for nothing more than faith that will keep asking even when we're confused, will keep seeking even when the road takes unexpected turns, and will keep knocking even when it feels as if the door is padlocked against us. In the scheme of eternity, Jesus promises the answer will speedily come.

As we walk in faith, we learn to embrace the incredible blessing of God's delight in us, something that has the power to motivate like nothing else. When we intercede, we realize that God is not concerned with whether our words are eloquent or inept, whether we pray one minute or sixty, whether we feel as if we can move a mountain or barely eke out a cry. Why? Because we know that His soul rejoices at our willingness to come to Him on behalf of another, for He sees it as an act of faith—the one thing He is looking for. Truly there is no greater reward than to experience this kind of pleasure from the almighty God.

LESSONS FROM MY OWN STORY

In the ten years that followed my receiving the message from the Lord that I shared at the beginning of this chapter, our church saw God do some wonderful things. We began to experience tastes of Christ's manifest presence as worship became an exciting adventure week after week. God catapulted our members across the world and throughout the streets of our community in joyful response

His soul rejoices at our willingness to come to Him on behalf of another, for He sees it as an act of faith—the one thing He is looking for.

to His call to go and make disciples. College students poured in by droves, seeking a church where they could live out their passionate desire to see Jesus lifted up. Truly it seemed God had begun to fulfill the promise He had given me. But always there was this nagging reminder in the back of my mind about the part concerning days of darkness. I began to hope that maybe I'd gotten that little bit wrong, for surely a flame was starting to burn brightly in my heart and the hearts of many others.

Then one day I sensed the Lord telling me to cull my prayer journals for everything He'd ever said about our ministry so I could share it with my husband. Skimming eleven years of journals, I was surprised to find more than thirty conversations the Lord and I had enjoyed, which added up to eight pages of things He seemed to have spoken directly to me. Most of the messages were a confirmation of the promise that we would see revival fires, but many messages spoke as well of those dark days to come. I was no longer able to dismiss the notion.

Within days after God called me to assimilate all His words, it seemed as if He closed the doors of heaven and stopped speaking to me altogether. After several months, I began to understand that I had entered what the saints of old called a "dark night of the soul"—one of those seasons where God's presence cannot be felt, His answers to prayer are not forthcoming, and His voice is completely silent. I knew then why God had given me that assignment, for over the course of the next two years, I found myself poring over those pages of promises again and again, pondering their message in light of the events that would take place.

LEARNING TO WRESTLE WITH GOD

Soon a sort of boldness began to characterize my prayers, and though at times I felt like someone stranded in the middle of a desert land, I wrestled with God as if He were standing right in front of me. Day after day as we went to the mat, I offered up my own pleas and those from the mouths of other intercessors in Scripture. Often I repeated David's cry: "Restore us, O God of our salvation, and cause Your indignation toward us to cease. Will You be angry with us forever? Will You prolong Your anger to all generations? Will You not Yourself revive us again, that Your people may rejoice in You?" (Psalm 85:4–6). I claimed various scriptural promises about prayer, telling God that these were Jesus's words, not mine, and that His name was on the line if He didn't come through. Though at times I felt a bit presumptuous, I believe I was touching on what it means to pray in Jesus's name or for His name's sake, something I was sure my Father God could not ignore.

One day I was stunned to read these words during my devotional time: "Put Me in remembrance, let us argue our case together; state your cause, that you may be proved right" (Isaiah 43:26). What could this mean? Why would

God want me to argue with Him like some kind of lawyer, just so I could be proved right? Then I remembered dinner conversations as a teenager with my own father, who often asked each of us what we had learned at school that day. Inevitably one of the five would be grilled in detail, my father playing the part of the devil's advocate as he challenged the things we said, giving rise to hearty debates. I look back now and realize that my dad delighted in the whole ordeal—not because he needed our wisdom, but because he enjoyed seeing his children process and ponder and interact with him as we tested our assumptions or strengthened our convictions.

It is a fascinating principle of intercession that God takes a unique pleasure in our willingness to "stand up to Him" with a well-thought-out case based upon principles in Scripture. This put a whole new spin for me on the story of the Canaanite woman who argued with Jesus about her son's right to be healed. I realized that He wasn't being condescending when He told her it was not good to take the children's bread and throw it to the dogs. He was simply engaging her in the process of wrestling with Him for the answer she so desperately needed. He must have been delighted when she insisted that even dogs get the crumbs off the table!

When we find ourselves praying in this way, we can feel like a nagging spouse or a complaining child, but God doesn't see it that way at all. As Donald Bloesch wrote: "Wrestling is not whining, for it springs from strength, not weakness. It means refusing to let go of God without a blessing."[6] God truly loves it when we try to pin Him down with our best moves again and again, determined that until He blesses us with some answers, we are not going to give up in our prayers for others.

DEALING WITH DIVINE DELAYS

At the heart of every divine delay is a purpose we cannot always see. As the months went by and the darkness remained, I found myself contemplating the stories of Abraham and Joseph and David and all that happened between the time God gave each of them a promise and the time He fulfilled it. Though I've often said *wait* may be God's favorite word, I understand now that every waiting room is really a preparation room. This may be why Jesus calls us to keep asking and seeking and knocking. There are things He needs to do—within us as well as within the people and the situations we are praying for—which can happen only over the course of time.

Have you ever wondered how many people waited for, longed for, and interceded for the coming of the Messiah? For hundreds of years the promise had been passed on from generation to generation, but Paul told us that "when the fullness of the time came, God sent forth His Son" (Galatians 4:4). I wonder, for example, if Anna, the prophetess who fasted and prayed for His coming for more than sixty years, understood how intricately God had put every detail in place to answer her cries the day she encountered the infant Messiah when Mary and Joseph brought Him to be dedicated.

Waiting is kind of like the birth process—there are things that must take place over the course of nine months to prepare that baby (and the parents as well) for entrance into this world. As intercessors, we may feel at times like a woman going through false labor. The contractions can seem so real that we're sure delivery is imminent, finding ourselves disappointed when the answers don't materialize. This happened to me many times throughout the course of my journey. I cannot tell you how often I felt absolutely certain that a breakthrough was about to take place, only to be proved mistaken again and again.

Here's the interesting thing about those Braxton Hicks contractions.[7] They are not some accident of nature or a false alarm designed to put a woman in a state of panic about the pregnancy. There is a very specific purpose in these contractions, and that is to prepare the body and baby for the real delivery. As intercessors, when we feel that we've been on the verge of giving birth time and again, we can remember that there is a reason for the delay—God is lining things up, putting all the pieces in place to deliver the miracle for which we've asked.

This solves the problem of wondering how long we should pray for something. As Wesley Duewel wrote: "There is often great mystery concerning the time span required in prevailing prayer. The secret of prevailing prayer is simply to pray until the answer comes. The length of time is ultimately immaterial. It is God's answer that counts."[8] Because God operates outside the confines of time, a thousand years is as a day to Him. Though it may seem as if we've waited an eternity, in the scheme of things the answer is only a breath away, and God in His sovereign wisdom knows when to release it into our care.

GROANS THAT CANNOT BE UTTERED

On the Sunday after September 11, 2001, my husband called for a spirit of repentance to fall upon our church body. Looking back, I'm not sure we knew what we were asking. God began to lay bare many hearts, including Joe's and mine, cutting away at our flesh like a skilled surgeon. A worship leader resigned after confessing to immorality, and an elder stepped down to deal with some deep anger toward God. Difficulties between the staff in our church began to surface that seemed to have little hope of being resolved. We watched helplessly as a steady trickle of people left our body for greener pastures elsewhere.

One Sunday morning before church as I was praying for our services, I found something welling up within me at a visceral level. Falling to my knees, I began to sob like a person in the throes of grief as I poured out my heart to the Lord without ever saying a word. I'm not sure how long the weeping lasted, but when the tears stopped, I opened my Bible to Romans 8 and understood for the first time what Paul meant when he wrote:

> If we hope for what we do not see, with perseverance we wait eagerly for it.
>
> In the same way the Spirit also helps our weakness;

for we do not know how to pray as we should, but the
Spirit Himself intercedes for us with groanings too deep
for words. (vv. 25–26)

Those groanings became a way of life for me in the following months. Our prayer garden was almost finished by
then, and night after night I would wander out there or lie
huddled in a blanket under the stars as I cried out to God
from the depths of my being. I'm not sure I can identify all
the Spirit was groaning about within me, but I have a good
idea. I believe the ache for revival in my heart was the very
grief God feels over the backslidden condition of His people,
and with every tear I shed, He was expressing His own
yearnings through me.

In one of Jeremiah's conversations with God, he asked
a question that became mine during that time: "Why has
my pain been perpetual and my wound incurable, refusing
to be healed? Will You indeed be to me like a deceptive
stream with water that is unreliable?" God's answer to
this discouraged prophet wrought hope within my soul—
I clung to it as someone drowning would hold on to a life-
line. "If you return, then I will restore you—before Me
you will stand; and if you extract the precious from the
worthless, you will become My spokesman" (Jeremiah
15:18–19).

I learned through that season of unutterable groaning
that the ministry of intercession could very well be more
about what God wanted to do in me than the results I
thought were so critical. Over and over again as I cried

before the Lord concerning the situations we faced, He would respond by showing me some other worthless place in my own soul from which He wanted to extract something precious for His glory.

I remember one night in particular when I lay weeping on my office floor before the Lord. Joe came in to try to help, but I told him there was no point; this was something between God and me and we'd have to work it out alone. After he left, I told the Lord He could have me, He could take whatever He wanted, that whether He ever answered another prayer, I was His. Like Solomon's bride combing the streets of the city, I was lovesick and yearned only for the return of my Beloved (Song 5:6–8).

Looking back on that night, I can tell you that something profound happened, something so sacred it's difficult to even write about it. Though it felt as if God were nowhere to be found, the memory of those moments still fills me with peace and a deep sense of spiritual sweetness. I can't explain it, but God was there more powerfully in His silence and absence than He'd ever been in the days of His tangible presence. Though I may not have understood it then, God Himself was carrying me with a tender love I doubt I'll ever fully grasp.

Many intercessors have known the sorrow that comes from long seasons of unanswered prayer. Some have cried out for

God was there more powerfully in His silence and absence than He'd ever been in the days of His tangible presence.

years for a lost spouse or a prodigal child. Others have pleaded at length for their church, only to see things get worse instead of better. Whatever the case may be, I have come to believe that these groanings of our hearts can be a fellowship with the sufferings of Jesus unlike any other. He is with us, and the work He is doing in extracting the precious from the worthless in our lives will bring great reward. This, too, is a gift that intercession offers to all who will remain through its dark night.

SCORPIONS AND SNAKES

It would have been hard in those days for me to imagine how things could get much worse, but in fact they did. For two years I had clung to God's promises from Scripture and those on the pages of my prayer journals, believing with each new struggle that the light would soon break through the cloudy confusion that had settled on us all. But instead, a series of events took place that resulted in one of the most painful experiences of our entire ministry as our church was split down the middle within a matter of a few weeks.

I will never forget the Sunday following a specially called congregational meeting in which my husband and the elders shared some difficult decisions they had made concerning four staff members. I stood at the back that day, greeting people as I'd done for more than twenty years. But as the service began, all I could think of was those who weren't there—friends we'd led to the Lord, members whose children we'd helped bring into the world and whose parents we'd helped bury, those we'd walked with through painful divorce and rebellious teenagers and broken hearts and a host of other critical life events—individuals who only a short time before had been like our very own family.

Over the course of the next few months, we felt like a church in mourning. For those who stayed and for those who left as well, it was an excruciating and confusing ordeal. We had been one body, free from any kind of major disharmony for more than twenty years, so how could this happen now? What could be so powerful as to sever us in two so quickly? It just didn't make sense.

Clinging to the remnant of faith I had, I kept waiting for a miracle to take place that would make everything clear and resolve things in some way that would show God's power even more. But as the weeks went by, hope began to grow dim. One day I read Jesus's familiar promise concerning prayer in Luke:

> Suppose one of you fathers is asked by his son for a fish; he will not give him a snake instead of a fish, will he? Or if he is asked for an egg, he will not give him a scorpion, will he? If you then, being evil, know how to give good gifts to your children, how much more will your heavenly Father give the Holy Spirit to those who ask Him? (11:11–13)

I pondered the words, asking the Lord how I could believe this passage—after all, wasn't the Holy Spirit exactly what I had been asking for all this time? I turned to the same promise in Matthew, who ended it a little differently, saying, "How much more will your Father who is in heaven give what is good to those who ask Him!" (Matthew 7:11). I felt then as if I could almost hear God asking, *Am I not good? Do I not give only good gifts? I promised you I wouldn't give you scorpions or snakes, so why do you act as if I have?*

There are going to be times when we, as intercessors, choose to stand in the gap, but the answers we receive don't look at all like what we've asked for, and in fact may seem just the opposite. A teenage daughter gets pregnant by the boy we've pleaded for God to take out of her life. A pastor for whom we've long interceded gets caught embezzling church funds. A lost neighbor for whom we've pounded the gates of heaven becomes offended and won't talk about God with us anymore.

To walk in faith requires that we receive these things and whatever may come to us as a gift from our Father's hand, and not give in to the lie that He's handed us scorpions and snakes instead. Clinging to the truth that God is always working things together for our good, we must stand in faith against the fiery darts the enemy will surely hurl during these seasons that seem like setbacks to the visions we've embraced in intercession.

OBTAINING A TESTIMONY

Two years have passed since those heartbreaking events, and I can say now that the suffering we endured has greatly strengthened my faith. I am more confident today than ever before that God will do what He has said He will do. As I write these thoughts, there are hopeful signs on the horizon. Pastors in our community are praying together regularly, and their members are joining in weeklong prayer vigils and multichurch praise events. This spring dozens of congregations in our area will prayer-walk to every home in our community to intercede for the coming of God's kingdom. Seeing these things stirs my heart with anticipation. Could the fulfillment of my soul's yearnings, the answer to my years of crying out, be on its way at last?

Honestly, I don't know. What I am sure of beyond a shadow of a doubt is that God is going to answer those prayers, or He wouldn't have given me His word and the faith to cling to it all these years. But I've read those pages of promises carefully, and the one thing they don't tell me is *when* the answer is going to come—it may or may not be in my lifetime. If it is, I can only imagine the joy that will be mine, along with all the precious believers who have interceded for revival in San Diego for so long. But if it isn't, then I will continue to rejoice in the Lord, for my goal is to die in faith. If I don't receive the promise here, I know I'll welcome it from that city whose architect and builder is God (Hebrews 11:10, 13).

On the roof of our church building, the ashes of a dear saint were once scattered—those of my aunt, the woman who challenged me to fall in love with Jesus when I was nineteen. Aunt Naomi loved Christ, for He had plucked her life from the pit and she had never gotten over being grateful. A little spitfire of a woman, we all adored her and gleaned from

> They are all around us, you know—men and women who have joined that great cloud of witnesses and who now cheer on you and me with every act of intercession.

her faith. Naomi longed for revival, and when she came to help us plant our church, it was her dream that this would be the place she'd see the Spirit poured out at last. I know that in her dying days she continued to cry out for it.

When I think of my own heart's desire, I often remember that long before my journey began, she was there, knocking faithfully on heaven's doors until the day God called her home. They are all around us, you know—men and women who have joined that great cloud of witnesses and who now cheer on you and me with every act of intercession. Scripture tells us that these precious souls—some who saw the fulfillment of their vision here on earth and others who didn't, but who gave their lives in faith trying to bring it about—each earned an honorable reputation with God in the process, obtaining a testimony in His sight (Hebrews 11). This is what matters most to me now and will be the desire of my heart for the rest of my days.

Oh, the beauty of faith. Think of it—in some unique way, we can gain an honorable reputation before God when no one else even cares. We can obtain a testimony in His sight whether or not anyone else ever sees our struggles. As intercessors, there is no more eloquent charge than the one that follows the great Hall of Faith in the book of Hebrews:

Since we have so great a cloud of witnesses surrounding us, let us also lay aside every encumbrance and the sin which so easily entangles us, and let us run with endurance the race that is set before us, fixing our eyes on Jesus, the author and perfecter of faith. (12:1–2)

PRACTICING PRAYER

Once again we will pause to meditate on the prayers of other saints. Here's a format you can follow, but feel free to establish your own:

- Read these prayers silently through once, pondering the heart and meaning in them.
- Read each one aloud, as if it were your own.
- Journal your thoughts about what you have read, then write your own prayer.
- Read your written prayer to the Lord aloud.

A PRAYER OF JEREMIAH FOR THE PEOPLE OF ISRAEL
(JEREMIAH 14:19–22 NLT)

LORD, have you completely rejected Judah? Do you really hate Jerusalem? Why have you wounded us past all hope of healing? We hoped for peace, but no peace came. We hoped for a time of healing but found only terror.

LORD, we confess our wickedness and that of our ancestors, too. We all have sinned against you. For the sake of your own name, LORD, do not abandon us. Do not disgrace yourself and the throne of your glory. Do not break your covenant with us. Please don't forget us!

Can any of the foreign gods send us rain? Does it fall from the sky by itself? No, it comes from you, the LORD our God! Only you can do such things. So we will wait for you to help us.

A PRAYER OF CHRISTINA ROSSETTI TITLED "A BETTER RESURRECTION"

Born in London in 1830, Christina Rossetti was one of the most important female poets of the nineteenth century. Christina's life of profound intimacy with Christ is reflected in the poems she wrote, including this one, which speaks of her own dark night.

I have no wit, no words, no tears;
My heart within me like a stone
Is numb'd too much for hopes or fears;
Look right, look left, I dwell alone;

I lift mine eyes, but dimm'd with grief
No everlasting hills I see;
My life is in the falling leaf:
O Jesus, quicken me.

My life is like a faded leaf,
My harvest dwindled to a husk:
Truly my life is void and brief
And tedious in the barren dusk;
My life is like a frozen thing,
No bud nor greenness can I see:
Yet rise it shall—the sap of Spring;
O Jesus, rise in me.

My life is like a broken bowl,
A broken bowl that cannot hold
One drop of water for my soul
Or cordial in the searching cold;
Cast in the fire the perish'd thing;
Melt and remould it, till it be
A royal cup for Him, my King:
O Jesus, drink of me.

Looking Ahead

The only fitting end for our journey together is to lift our eyes and set our sights on the unseen world where Christ reigns at the right hand of His Father. I am convinced that a clear and supernatural vision of God's plan to sum up all things in the person of His Son can be the most dramatic motivating force we'll ever find for a life of intercession. What little God has enabled me to grasp of this has shaped and molded me and become a powerful prism through which I now seek to view every aspect of my life. It has made intercession a profound wonder, and though I know I can never do the subject justice, I hope you'll gather with me around the throne.

CHAPTER SEVEN

AROUND THE THRONE

---

*The Joy of Interceding with
Eternity in Our Hearts*

---

*A view of God upon His throne will
make us think His service our privilege,
His precepts our ornaments, and obedience to Him the greatest honor and
nobility. It will make us weighty and
serious in our performances: it would
stake us down to any duty.*

STEPHEN CHARNOCK[1]

What is heaven like? In what has become a classic exploration of people's near-death experiences, Dr. Raymond Moody investigated one hundred case studies in which each subject had survived "clinical death" with a story to relate of what they had seen. He found their tales surprisingly similar, most of which included sensations of light, feelings of warmth, and assurances of unconditional love. Since the book was first published in 1975, the subject has spawned what can be described only as a religion based upon NDEs or near-death experiences.

As compelling and otherworldly as these stories sound, they bear little resemblance to what the Bible calls the third heaven—that spiritual dimension into which Paul was caught up, but forbidden to speak of. What do we know about this place that he referred to as paradise?[2] Scripture offers us some fascinating information, much of which is based on the experiences of various writers who, like Paul, were given a glimpse into the mysteries of heaven that every believer is destined to one day enjoy.

If we were to interview these folks, their stories would be very different from those of Moody's study subjects. For example, instead of soothing assurances of unconditional love, Isaiah might talk about feeling ruined by his own sin when he saw the Lord sitting on a throne, lofty and exalted. Instead of pleasant sensations of warmth, Ezekiel might tell us that when the heavens opened up to reveal a blazing throne bearing a man who glowed like molten metal, the radiance was such that all he could do was fall flat on his face.[3]

Our most fascinating look into this unspeakable spiritual dimension comes from the apostle John, to whom the exalted Christ appeared while he was in exile on the Isle of Patmos. At first glance John also fainted away like a dead man, but after Jesus tenderly reassured him and imparted messages for seven churches, Revelation tells us that he saw a door standing open in heaven. When a trumpetlike voice beckoned him to come up and see the things that were to take place, John gladly acquiesced.

What do you suppose might have been the thing that grabbed his attention as he stepped through that door? From the vast expanse that opened before John's eyes, what would you imagine he'd be compelled to speak of first? John tells us that he was immediately in the Spirit, and then, with an almost breathtaking sense of awe, he declared, "And behold, a throne was standing in heaven, and One sitting on the throne" (Revelation 4:2). Even as I write this, I feel a hush fall over me, as if I'm treading on holy ground.

Behold, a throne . . . Stop for a moment and ponder these three words, for they are the reality that circumscribes the annals of history and transcends the bonds of time. This truth encompasses the existence of every king who has ever ruled and every nation that has ever been trampled down or that will ever exercise dominion over another. All the activity of planet Earth—every birth and breath and death—has first passed through the hands of the sovereign Ruler who holds court there even now. Nothing so defines our reason for living or clarifies the hope of our calling like the truth that our King reigns eternally and supremely. *Behold, a throne.*

That this perspective ought to give us pause is a driving theme throughout Scripture. The psalmist wrote, "The LORD reigns, let the peoples tremble; He is enthroned above the cherubim, let the earth shake!" (Psalm 99:1). God declared through the prophet Isaiah, "Heaven is My throne and the earth is My footstool. Where then is a house you could build for Me? And where is a place that I may rest?" (Isaiah 66:1). When we consider these things, we can only bow and ask, as David did, "What is man that You take thought of him?" (Psalm 8:4).

Though you and I will not personally experience all that John saw until we reach heaven's gates ourselves, I believe we can glean much from this grand finale of God's written Word. There are treasures hidden in this

All the activity of planet Earth—every birth and breath and death—has first passed through the hands of the sovereign Ruler who holds court there even now.

> Do you live with an awareness that in this very moment there are vats surrounding the throne of God that are filled with every prayer you and I and all believers throughout history have ever prayed?

revelation that have the power to completely transform the way we view our call to pray.

In one of John's descriptions of the worship around the throne, he wrote of the twenty-four elders who held a harp and golden bowls full of incense, which, he tells us, are "the prayers of the saints." Do you see this? Do you live with an awareness that in this very moment there are vats surrounding the throne of God that are filled with every prayer you and I and all believers throughout history have ever prayed? Think of it—no plea is ever lost, no act of intercession ever ignored, the sounds of our hearts' cries cannot die out over time. Instead, the aroma of each request—the great and small, lengthy and short, lofty and mundane—rises continually to saturate the atmosphere of heaven and bring pleasure to God, our King (Revelation 5:8; 8:4).

This is the reality that has captivated my heart as an intercessor. In this final chapter I long to bring forth the splendor of this scene in a manner worthy of the exalted Christ, who is seated in glory there. I am convinced that once the eyes of our hearts are opened to this, we cannot help but be struck with awe every time we engage in an act of intercession. To that end, journey with me to explore the sights and sounds of a place that is truly beyond imagination, but that we will one day call home.

A THRONE OF GLORY

Above all else, the throne room of God reverberates with displays of glory. To capture the spectrum of events and beings that John saw in his heavenly vision would put Hollywood's finest movie producers to the test. From pulsing flashes of light to resounding peals of thunder, from six-winged creatures with eyes on every side to the seraphim who dart to and fro like burning torches, from a crystal sea below to an emerald rainbow above—the throne room of God is a place to stagger the senses. Yet none of these things even begin to compare to the marvel of the centerpiece of heaven, the One who sits on His throne of glory (Isaiah 63:15; Matthew 25:31). There our Lord radiates forth the full display of His being, something we cannot even begin to comprehend.

Whenever God reveals His glory on earth, it seems to affect people in extraordinary ways. It caused the Israelites to stand at a distance and tremble, and Moses had to cover his face with a veil to keep those who looked at him from going blind as he came out from the presence of the Lord. On one occasion, Scripture tells us, the priests couldn't stand up to minister in the temple because the glory of God was so strong, and on another they couldn't even enter the house of the Lord.[4]

In each of these situations there was only a partial revelation of God's glory, so just imagine what it must be like to be in His very presence. Words are inadequate, our loftiest thoughts surely fall short, and yet we can't help but try to fathom the wonder our destiny foretells. I once heard Joni

Eareckson Tada, the amazing woman who has dedicated her life as a paraplegic to shining forth the love of Christ, tell how she envisions such a scene. Surmising that because God knows we could never handle seeing Him on full display, Joni suggests that He will choose one facet of glory at a time to unveil. When He shines it forth, all the inhabitants of heaven will gasp and fall back in awe, where we will remain for about two hundred years. Then God will disclose some other facet of His glory, and once again all in attendance will fall back in awe . . . for another two hundred years. Because God is infinitely glorious and there is no end to the attributes He could reveal, Joni suggests that this process can only continue throughout eternity.

When I was a teenager, my family visited Calvary Baptist Church in San Diego several times just to listen to the great black orator Shadrach Meshach Lockridge. In my entire life I have never heard anyone who could paint the glories of eternity as this man did. Even now I can see him standing, eyes rolled toward heaven, deep voice booming as every person in that church—young and old, rich and poor, black and white—sat spellbound. I remember one time in particular when he shared the story of the world, ending with a plea for people to respond to the way Christ had made for sinners through His death and resurrection. As he bellowed again and again, "The door is open; the door is open," it seemed as if the entire congregation was going to storm the altar where he stood.

In one of his messages that has since become a beloved classic throughout Christendom, Pastor Lockridge began with these words:

My King was born King. The Bible says He's a Seven Way King. He's the King of the Jews—that's a racial King. He's the King of Israel—that's a national King. He's the King of righteousness. He's the King of the ages. He's the King of heaven. He's the King of glory. He's the King of kings and He is the Lord of lords. Now that's my King. Well I wonder if you know Him. Do you know Him?[5]

Though the content of this sermon is poetic and deeply eloquent, you begin to sense that Reverend Lockridge felt a certain frustration in trying to get his point across. After almost eighty profound statements about the exalted Christ, he finally paused to say, "Well, I wish I could describe Him to you, but He's indescribable. He's indescribable. Yes. He's incomprehensible." Clearly Lockridge had spent a fair amount of time pondering the majestic halls of heaven where the King of glory reigns.

A view of the throne of glory provides an amazing backdrop for intercession. Because we are seated in heavenly places even now, we no longer stand looking up like beggars who yearn for the goods that we know are there (Ephesians 2:6). Instead, as joint heirs with Christ, we look down upon the earth and take heart that every need we see can be met with the riches that surround us. As we gaze at God's glory, we understand that His every attribute can uniquely affect what we pray and how we pray.

We see His sovereign rule and know that since He answers to no one, our King won't need permission to use His

> Because we are seated in heavenly places even now, we no longer stand looking up like beggars who yearn for the goods that we know are there (Ephesians 2:6).

authority to fulfill our requests as He sees fit. We envision myriad upon myriad of angels running to do His bidding, and we are humbled that He is personally attuned to every cause we bring before Him. We hear the living creatures and elders crying, "Holy, holy, holy is the Lord God Almighty," and take comfort in knowing that He answers our pleas with purity and integrity and in perfect righteousness. As Charles Spurgeon once preached:

> In prayer we stand where angels bow with veiled faces. There, even there, the cherubim and seraphim adore before that selfsame throne to which our prayers ascend. And should we come there with stunted requests and narrow and contracted faith?[6]

A true vision of the throne of glory has the power to turn weak pleas into bold affirmations, hesitant requests into passionate desires, and wishful thinking into faith-filled declarations.

THRONE OF GRACE

But ah, blessed wonder—the throne of glory is also a throne of grace. It is an amazing truth that our Lord is filled with tender compassion for those of us who will one day inhabit His glorious home. The book of Isaiah tells us that even now God is preparing a lavish banquet, which He Himself will serve as He removes the covering of glory, which without His grace would completely destroy us. Isaiah wrote:

> He will swallow up death for all time,
> And the Lord God will wipe tears away from all faces,
> And He will remove the reproach of His people from all
>   the earth;
> For the Lord has spoken. (25:8)

The God of glory burns with love for His redeemed. The fulfillment of this promise is shown two different times in John's vision (Revelation 7:17; 21:4). The Son of God longs for the day He will be able to take His beloved bride in His arms and wipe away every tear as He restores us to the beauty that reflects His very own.

Perhaps one of the most poignant interchanges John witnessed was when the time came to break the seals of the book that would usher in the final judgments that must take place. When it appeared as if there was no one worthy in all of heaven and earth to open the book, John began to weep. Soon, an elder called for him to look up, saying, "Stop weeping; behold, the Lion that is from the tribe of Judah, the Root of David, has overcome so

> The God of glory burns with love for His redeemed.

as to open the book and its seven seals" (Revelation 5:5). Then, John wrote, "I saw between the throne (with the four living creatures) and the elders a Lamb standing, as if slain" (v. 6). Within the context of this short interchange we see three pictures of Christ—the Lion, the Root, and the Lamb—that explain why the eternal I AM reigns from a throne of grace.

The exalted Christ is the Lion from the tribe of Judah, a description that harks back to the time when Jacob prophesied over his son Judah likening him to a young lion that would one day overpower his enemies and earn the adulation of all his brothers. Hundreds of years later these words were fulfilled as the tribe of Judah stormed into Canaan, carrying a banner etched with the likeness of a lion to stake a claim on land for all the other tribes.[7]

Scripture tells us that in this same way Jesus, who hails from the tribe of Judah, is a forerunner for us, for He has entered within the veil of God's presence, securing a home there for every redeemed child (Hebrews 6:19–20). And what kind of banner did He carry as He defeated death's curse and vanquished the enemy of our souls? In the beautiful picture of Christ and the church found in the Song of Solomon, we discover that the Bridegroom, who brings His beloved to His banqueting table, holds over her a banner of love (Song 2:4).

When we intercede on behalf of others, we must remember that because we come to a throne of grace, our Lord the Lion now stands in strength and victory, waving His banner of love over their hearts. Like the armies of Israel who would not give up until every tribe had fully inhabited their own plot of land, we go wherever Christ has staked a claim and fight until we see His beloved receiving the tender mercies with which He ever longs to shower them.

Jesus is also the Root of David, a reminder that we serve a covenant-keeping God. Isaiah foretold that a Messiah would come from the stem of Jesse, David's father, and dozens of Old Testament prophecies promised that of His throne there would be no end. The emerald rainbow that surrounds the throne John saw beckons us to believe that because Christ has bought us with His blood, we live within a covenant of grace with the Almighty.

When we stand in the gap on behalf of our mothers and brothers and friends and foes alike, we rest assured that we do not pray to a capricious God, but to One who always keeps His word. Because He is bound to us through a covenant of grace, we know that there is nothing we must do to earn His intervention—we need only come. Though delays may discourage and detours dim our hopes, we can cling to the truth that because He is the Root of David, "as many as are the promises of God, in Him they are yes" (Isaiah 11:1; 2 Corinthians 1:20).

Perhaps no vision can more powerfully shape our intercession than that of the Lamb who was slain. When we pray, we see Jesus dying, not for the world in some vague and general way, but for that friend whose heart has been hard for as long as we can

Our Lord the Lion now stands in strength and victory, waving His banner of love over their hearts.

remember. When we cry out, we hear Christ's voice of forgiveness, not only for the saints we find easy to love, but also for
rebellious children and arrogant bosses and angry neighbors.

Standing in the gap on behalf of someone else can
become for you and me an act of communion—a time to
remember the price Christ has paid and to give thanks.
Because of the Lamb who was slain, we draw near with confidence to the throne of grace, ever looking for mercy and
grace for those we lift up in prayer in their time of need
(Hebrews 4:16).

A Throne of Worship

It almost goes without saying that the throne of God is a
place of worship, for what else can creatures do when confronted with the glories of the One who made them for His
own pleasure? John's vision is saturated with the sounds of
worship. Like punctuation marks in the story, his story
regales us with the praises of those gathered there on five
different occasions. In *The Message*, Eugene Peterson's powerful paraphrase of Scripture, he captures the sense of awe
John must have felt as he came to the final outcry:

> Then I heard the sound of massed choirs, the sound of a
> mighty cataract, the sound of strong thunder:
>
> Hallelujah!
> The Master reigns,
>   our God, the Sovereign-Strong!

Let us celebrate, let us rejoice,

    let us give him the glory! (Revelation 19:6–7)

Oh, that the present reality of this would so consume us that a day could never pass without our pondering its significance for the decisions we make and the actions we take and the prayers we offer on behalf of our fallen world. This very moment our King is being worshiped, honored, glorified, and esteemed in the halls of heaven—by saints who've gone before us, by angelic hosts, by elders, and by living creatures who can only bow and sing in antiphonal chorus of His breathtaking holiness.

Contemplating Christ as the glorified One has profoundly impacted how I pray, for it shapes and informs my requests. I am keenly aware, for example, that whatever difficulties a person may face, Christ is still worthy to be exalted as Lord in their hearts. At the same time I realize that the people I pray for may not have experienced the wonder of a God who wants to meet them in the midst of their struggles. So, whether I intercede over a broken marriage or a lonely child, a shattered church or a cancer-ridden neighbor, an agnostic friend or a faithful pastor, I ask that Christ will *manifest* Himself to them in some way so that they will *magnify* Him as He deserves. In the face of devastating needs or perplexing difficulties, I can always pray, "Come, Lord Jesus, come— make Yourself real; exalt Yourself in this situation."

A great Chinese martyr once suggested that all prayer is communing with Christ for the manifestation of His glory. I believe this will become true for each of us to the degree that

In the face of devastating needs or perplexing difficulties, I can always pray, "Come, Lord Jesus, come—make Yourself real; exalt Yourself in this situation."

we spend time at the throne of worship. The deeper we drink of the glory in that place, the more we will be driven to cry out for others to experience it as well. The more we see Christ's infinite worth as He reigns on high, the more we will yearn for Him to be exalted in the hearts of those for whom we pray. This is the highest form of intercession, for it pleases our Father, who lives to see every knee bow in adoration before His Son.

THE FULFILLMENT OF ALL THINGS

For most of my Christian walk, my vision for intercession was a fairly narrow one. Though at times I prayed for lost souls in my city or missionaries who might be passing through, I had no idea that my destiny was wrapped up in something far beyond my small slice of life. Because I somehow missed the message that God has been in pursuit of a very specific agenda from the beginning of time, I was ignorant of the ways in which He has called me to be a part of that process. I did not know that God is filling this earth with His glory as the waters cover the sea—not by saving souls in some random fashion, but through a plan that unfolds on page after page of Scripture (Habakkuk 2:14). What is it? We need look no further than another aspect of the scene in John's throne-room vision. He wrote:

> After these things I looked, and behold, a great multitude which no one could count, from every nation and all tribes and peoples and tongues, standing before the throne and before the Lamb, clothed in white robes, and palm branches were in their hands; and they cry out with a loud voice, saying, "Salvation to our God who sits on the throne, and to the Lamb." (Revelation 7:9–10)

This picture lifts our eyes to the fulfillment of all things and assures us of something very important. When time is no more and saints gather at the feet of Jesus, there will be worshipers there from every single tribe and tongue that inhabits this earth. For those who understand this glorious certainty and choose to embrace a vision of intercession for the nations of the earth, a profound and incomparable joy awaits them.

A couple of years ago I went on a short-term mission trip to Bangladesh. After traveling twenty-four hours by plane, six by train, two by car, and finally twenty minutes on foot, I finally reached the remote village where I would share about Jesus with those who had never even heard His name. On my second day there, my translator became ill, leaving me to fend for myself among people with whom I had no way of communicating. After I prayer-walked the outskirts of the village, my

> When time is no more and saints gather at the feet of Jesus, there will be worshipers there from every single tribe and tongue that inhabits this earth.

The longing of my heart to be a part of bringing that great host of worshipers from every tribe and tongue to my Lord is a work that He has done because this is His passion and has been His plan from the beginning of time.

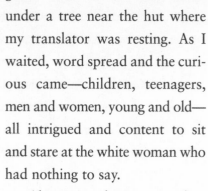

guide motioned for me to sit under a tree near the hut where my translator was resting. As I waited, word spread and the curious came—children, teenagers, men and women, young and old— all intrigued and content to sit and stare at the white woman who had nothing to say.

Alternating between smiling at their faces and taking in the vast tropical terrain, I quietly asked the Lord what in the world I was doing there. I thought about all the money, time, training, planning, and prayer that had been invested in this trip, and how at this moment I had the perfect opportunity to share the good news, but no means of doing so. (This would have been a great opportunity for God to enable me to speak with new tongues, but that didn't seem to be His plan.) As the afternoon slowly crept by, I passed the time singing praise songs softly under my breath, speaking words of Jesus's worth over this land held hostage by centuries of idolatry.

Soon deep and abiding joy began to flood my soul, and my heart soared to another scene. In my mind's eye, I saw not only this tribe, but all the peoples of the earth joining in colossal chorus to adore the Lamb upon His throne. Tears filled my eyes as I savored a tiny taste of that glorious moment for which all of history is headed. Though I could not speak the language of that particular people group, I could worship and pray for Christ's kingdom to come in that place, living out in some measure the end for which I was created.

I share this story for one reason. God has done something in my heart as an intercessor that I could never have done for myself—He has instilled in me a passion to see His name lifted high in every corner of this earth. Though the Lord has not called my husband and me to serve on a foreign field, rarely does a week go by that I don't find myself filled with deep yearning for His purposes across the globe. I can't explain it, but the mere mention of some missionary quests can move me to tears.

But here's what you must know: This didn't happen because I decided to get serious about evangelizing the world or determined to devote myself to reaching those who've never heard. I didn't become mission-minded by attending a conference or reading a book. The longing of my heart to be a part of bringing that great host of worshipers from every tribe and tongue to my Lord is a work that He has done because this is His passion and has been His plan from the beginning of time. The more I have learned to gaze upon Christ, seated on His throne and surrounded by that multi-racial crowd of worshipers, the deeper God has branded my heart with His own desire for the nations.

The End from the Beginning

I believe God lays forth that scene in John's vision so that each of us will live out our purpose as those who know the end from the beginning. John Piper wrote that "God's great goal

> To every one of us who professes faith in His name, Jesus invites us to join Him in the ministry of intercession for His global purposes.

in all of history is to uphold and display the glory of his name for the enjoyment of his people from all the nations."[8] Though it would be impossible to articulate all the ways this truth saturates Scripture, let me paint some broad strokes.[9] When God first told Abraham that through his seed all the *families* (another word for *nations*) of the world would be blessed, He had already put in place every detail to prepare for the fulfillment of that promise through His Son's death and resurrection. In His final farewell, Jesus commanded His followers to go into all the world and make disciples, instructing them to wait until the outpouring of power that would ensure He would have witnesses of the gospel even to the uttermost parts of the earth. The early church was on mission from the start to spread the truth, believing Christ's promise that His return hinged on every tribe and tongue having heard the good news (Matthew 24:14).

Here's the exciting part, the truth we just cannot miss: It is a very simple thing to be a part of advancing this incredible plan. God extends to each of us a clear call—for some to go and some to send and some to get the word out at home and some to give liberally and any number of other possibilities. But to every one of us who professes faith in His name, Jesus invites us to join Him in the ministry of intercession for His global purposes. We need only breathe in the atmosphere of heaven to catch the import of this glorious call to intercessors.

We saw earlier how our prayers are like incense that rises continually to the Father's throne, but there is something very unique about these aromatic strains. To grasp the wonder of this, we need to understand the role of incense in Scripture. The first time we read of it is when God appeared to Moses on Mount Sinai and gave him the instructions for the ministry of the priests, establishing that they were to burn it morning and night throughout all generations on a special altar in the tabernacle. The priest was to stand before God at these two times each day to minister to Him and bless His name while offering incense on behalf of the people who knelt outside in silent prayer. The fragrance of those finely ground spices as they burned were to be a perpetual reminder that prayer rising to the throne was a pleasing aroma to the Lord.[10]

Later, in one of the visions God gave to Isaiah, He explained that prayer, night and day, was to be the very heartbeat of temple activity—not just for the Jews, but for others as well. Speaking of how even foreigners would be brought into His "house of prayer" and made joyful as they ministered to Him, God proclaimed, "My house will be called a house of prayer for all the peoples" (Isaiah 56:7). That it had become a marketplace instead infuriated Jesus, who swept through the temple hundreds of years later, quoting Isaiah's prophecy as He overturned the tables of those who'd denigrated His holy dwelling place (Mark 11:15–18).

In the final book of the Old Testament, God once more reiterates the promise that there will come a time when the aroma of prayer—like incense offered in every place—will promote the greatness of His name among the nations. He says:

> From the rising of the sun even to its setting, My name will be great among the nations, and in every place incense is going to be offered to My name . . . for My name will be great among the nations. (Malachi 1:11)

BECOMING A HOUSE OF PRAYER

Some might suggest that the fulfillment of this and hundreds of other Old Testament prophecies began the afternoon Peter was given the vision that resulted in his accompanying three strangers to the house of Cornelius, an Italian army officer. There, as he preached, the power of God fell and the first group of non-Jews was converted to Christ. A short time later a hullabaloo arose among the rest of the disciples concerning what should be required of these Gentiles and others who had since come to faith. In the course of that discussion, James reminded the apostles that the fact that God would call people from groups outside the Jewish culture to be His own possession was something the prophets had foretold. Quoting Amos, he declared:

> With this the words of the Prophets agree, just as it is written, "After these things I will return, and I will rebuild the tabernacle of David which has fallen, and I will rebuild its ruins, and I will restore it, so that the rest

of mankind may seek the Lord, and all the Gentiles who are called by My name," says the Lord, who makes these things known from long ago. (Acts 15:15–18)

Herein lies the powerful connection for intercessors. As Christ's body, we are the tabernacle of David that is being rebuilt into a house of prayer for the nations, which God has always intended His dwelling place to be. Every time you or I offer up intercession for the gospel to go forth where it has not been proclaimed, we are fulfilling God's passion and causing Him great delight. How very extraordinary.

But there's more! Consider this mind-boggling thought: It is possible that our intercession for the nations might actually cause Christ to come back sooner! Peter told us to look for and hasten the coming day of God (2 Peter 3:12). Because we have seen the end from the beginning through John's glorious throne-room revelation, we know that hastening the day of Christ's return becomes the privilege of all who choose to participate in the spread of the gospel to every tribe and tongue on this planet.

And so we pray—for missionaries and unreached people groups and persecuted believers who daily give their lives to see Jesus's name proclaimed where it has not yet been heard. Do you grasp what a high calling even one little prayer—for an Indian evangelist or a Moroccan martyr

It is possible that our intercession for the nations might actually cause Christ to come back sooner!

or a Syrian pastor or an African village—can be? Though I cannot understand it, the thought that a request I might make could bring me face-to-face with my Lord even one second sooner stirs me to intercede for tribes and tongues who've yet to be reached.

Praying for the nations of the world can seem a daunting task until we remember that we need intercede only as our heavenly Father leads. There are so many opportunities—from Web sites to missionary newsletters, from fasts with a special focus to magazines about martyrs. Even our daily newspaper can be a source for intercession as we read of things that are happening across the globe. The key is not to try to take on the entire world, but perhaps one corner of it at a time—one tribe or a missionary from your home church or a country that happens to be in the news. And with every whisper of a request, even as the words leave our lips, we can be confident it is a pleasing aroma to the Lord as it moves our world closer to the fulfillment of all things in the worship of Jesus Christ.

I CAN ONLY IMAGINE

In 1991 a young songwriter named Bart Millard was deeply impacted by the loss of his father to cancer. Because his dad had assured him as he lay dying that he was getting the better end of the deal by going to be with the Lord, Bart found himself pondering the mysteries of eternity after his father was gone. For months he scribbled the words "I can only imagine" on any scrap of paper that happened to be available. Some eight years later, while traveling home from a concert with his band, Bart came across those scribbled words and within ten minutes had written an entire song asking what it would be like to enter heaven and stand face-to-face with Jesus.

The song was an immediate hit among Christian circles, winning several Dove awards, including the coveted Song of the Year award in 2002. But what happened next was something no one could have planned. It began one morning in January 2003 at a secular Dallas radio station when one member of a disc-jockey team, known for their outrageous antics, dared another, saying: "Are you crazy enough to play this song?" knowing that it was unlike anything else on the show's current playlist. The other DJ took up the dare, and within minutes callers began to flood the station's phone lines, requesting the song be played again and asking for more information about it.[11]

When the Dallas station responded by playing it regularly, a vice president at Curb Records in Los Angeles heard about it. Soon his company partnered with another to promote the single to mainstream radio, and the rest, as they say, is history. Garnering record-breaking airplay, the single remained first on Billboard Music's top singles sales chart for more than ten weeks, while the sales of the album that included the song soon soared to over one million.

What was it about this song that so captivated believers and nonbelievers alike? Some have attributed its success to America's hunger for hope in the aftermath of September 11. Others have suggested that this phenomenon proved at last that mainstream radio listeners would appreciate strong

What can a beggar
give a king?

Christian lyrics, if they just got the chance to hear them.

Whatever the answer might be, clearly there was something about the scenario the young songwriter posed that struck an unprecedented chord in the hearts of millions. In the chorus, he raises numerous possibilities about his future encounter with Christ. Will he dance? Will he fall to his knees? Will awe render him speechless? Will he sing hallelujah? To each question, Bart answers wistfully, "I can only imagine."

I, too, have pondered these things. I've pored over the book of Revelation and pictured my place there. I've studied the symbolism in the emerald rainbow and the sea of glass, and I've meditated on the detailed description of the exalted Christ that John provides. I've contemplated the faces of neighbors and friends and family and fellow saints across the globe, envisioning us all as we kneel in adoration, singing "Holy, holy, holy" at our Father's feet. This has become the stuff of life for me, that which can elevate even my most mundane tasks on any given day.

But throughout my imaginings, there is one question that tugs at me, one thought that captures my attention again and again. It is this: When I meet my beloved Redeemer, everything within me will long to have something to give Him, some token that might speak of my adoration for all that He is, my appreciation for all that He has done for me. But what can a beggar give a king? How can a sinner hope to bless the heart of an infinitely holy God? What could I possibly offer to the One from whom I have drawn my every life's breath?

And then I remember. God in His tender mercy and sovereign wisdom has already planned for this. For you and for me, He has fashioned an unfading crown of glory that awaits us even now. Paul wrote of this imperishable crown, comparing it to the wreath that the winner in an Olympic event received. In the same way, the crown Christ will award us on Judgment Day will represent the race we've run for the glory of His name. Surely many of those precious stones will have been perfected in the crucible of intercession. Can you fathom this? That by God's grace alone, the answers to the prayers He has inspired and enabled us to offer up will be like jewels to adorn us, ever casting their brilliant beams across the expanse of eternity?

John told us that the elders who surround Jesus on His throne are bedecked with crowns, but when confronted with all Christ's reigning glory, they have no recourse but to take them off and cast them down before Him as they fall to their knees in worship. This has become my moment of destiny—the sacred scene I often ponder. How it will happen, I don't know, but I envision a moment when, for me, time will stand still as the King of glory looks out across the host of

I envision a moment when, for me, time will stand still as the King of glory looks out across the host of faces before Him and pauses to fix His gaze upon me.

faces before Him and pauses to fix His gaze upon me. Though there will surely be a time for running and weeping and laughing and dancing, I believe that in the instant my Beloved's eyes meet mine, I will be able to do nothing else but cast my crown at His feet and worship my precious Redeemer. How I long for that day, when I will join those elders to proclaim:

> Worthy are You, our Lord and our God, to receive glory and honor and power; for You created all things, and because of Your will they existed, and were created. (Revelation 4:11)

Ah, the profound mystery of intercession—that there is eternal reward in every prayer we pray, a promise that we'll have something to give back to our Lord when we see Him face-to-face. And what a marvel that even now our simple prayers are a delightful fragrance filling heaven and blessing the God of the universe. These are the things that make my call as an intercessor a holy wonder, an unspeakable privilege, a perpetual wellspring of sacred joy—the depths of which I can only imagine.

PRACTICING PRAYER

Once again we will pause to meditate on the prayers of other saints. Here's a format you can follow, but feel free to establish your own:

- Read these prayers silently through once, pondering the heart and meaning in them.
- Read each one aloud, as if it were your own.
- Journal your thoughts about what you have read, then write your own prayer.
- Read your written prayer to the Lord aloud.

THE PRAYERS OF THOSE GATHERED AROUND THE THRONE
(ADAPTED FROM REVELATION 4:8, 11; 5:9–10, 12–14; 7:10–12; 11:17–18; 15:3–4; 19:1–4, 6–7; 22:20)

THE FOUR LIVING CREATURES: Holy, holy, holy is the Lord God, the Almighty, who was and who is and who is to come.

THE TWENTY-FOUR ELDERS: Worthy are You, our Lord and our God, to receive glory and honor and power; for You created all things, and because of Your will they existed, and were created.

THE LIVING CREATURES AND THE ELDERS: Worthy are You to take the book and to break its seals; for You were slain, and purchased for God with Your blood men from every tribe and tongue and people and nation. You have made them to be a kingdom and priests to our God; and they will reign upon the earth.

MYRIADS OF MYRIADS OF ANGELS: Worthy is the Lamb that

was slain to receive power and riches and wisdom and might and honor and glory and blessing.

EVERY CREATED THING: To Him who sits on the throne, and to the Lamb, be blessing and honor and glory and dominion forever and ever.

THE FOUR LIVING CREATURES: Amen.

A GREAT MULTITUDE FROM EVERY NATION, TRIBE, PEOPLE, AND TONGUE: Salvation to our God who sits on the throne, and to the Lamb.

THE ANGELS, ELDERS, AND LIVING CREATURES: Amen, blessing and glory and wisdom and thanksgiving and honor and power and might, be to our God forever and ever. Amen.

THE TWENTY-FOUR ELDERS: We give You thanks, O Lord God, the Almighty, who are and who were, because You have taken Your great power and have begun to reign. And the nations were enraged, and Your wrath came, and the time came for the dead to be judged, and the time to reward Your bond-servants the prophets and the saints and those who fear Your name, the small and the great, and to destroy those who destroy the earth.

THOSE WHO WERE VICTORIOUS OVER THE BEAST: Great and marvelous are Your works, O Lord God, the Almighty; righteous and true are Your ways, King of the nations! Who will not fear, O Lord, and glorify Your name? For You alone are holy; for all the nations will come and worship before You, for Your righteous acts have been revealed.

A GREAT MULTITUDE: Hallelujah! Salvation and glory and power belong to our God; because His judgments are true and righteous; for He has judged the great harlot

who was corrupting the earth with her immorality, and
He has avenged the blood of His bond-servants on her.
Hallelujah! Her smoke rises up forever and ever.

THE TWENTY-FOUR ELDERS AND THE FOUR LIVING CREATURES:
Amen. Hallelujah!

A GREAT MULTITUDE: Hallelujah! For the Lord our God, the
Almighty, reigns. Let us rejoice and be glad and give the
glory to Him, for the marriage of the Lamb has come
and His bride has made herself ready.

JESUS: Yes, I am coming quickly.

JOHN: Amen. Come, Lord Jesus.

A PRAYER OF THE
MISSIONARIES OF CHARITY

*The Missionaries of Charity is the Catholic order begun by
Mother Teresa—men and women who devote their lives to
caring for the poorest of the poor in this world. This is a
prayer they commonly offer after Communion, taken from
the Missionaries of Charity prayer book.*[12]

Dear Jesus, help us to spread your fragrance every-
where we go.
Flood our souls with your spirit and life.
Penetrate and possess our whole being,
so utterly,

that our lives may only be a radiance of yours.
Shine through us,
and be so in us,
that every soul we come in contact with
may feel your presence in our soul.
Let them look up and see no longer us
but only Jesus!
Stay with us,
and then we shall begin to shine as you shine;
so to shine as to be a light to others;
the light, O Jesus, will be all from you,
none of it will be ours;
it will be you, shining on others through us.
Let us thus praise you in the way you love best
by shining on those around us.
Let us preach you without preaching,
not by words but by our example,
by the catching force,
the sympathetic influence of what we do,
the evident fullness of the love our hearts bear
to you. Amen.

NOTES

CHAPTER ONE: IN SEARCH OF A DEFINITION

1. Mark Buchanan, *The Holy Wild* (Sisters, OR: Multnomah, 2004), 245.
2. Genesis 24:12–14; 25:19–23; 48–49; Ruth 2:12; 1 Kings 13:6; Job 42:7–10; 1 Chronicles 21:7–8.
3. Luke 22:31–32; John 17:20–23; 11:41–42; Luke 23:34; 24:50–53.
4. Acts 28:7–8; Romans 10:1; Romans 15:5; Ephesians 1:18–21; Colossians 1:9–10; 2 Thessalonians 1:11.
5. Romans 15:30; 2 Thessalonians 3:1–3; Philemon 22; Romans 15:32–33; Colossians 4:2–4; 2 Thessalonians 3:1.
6. Acts 7:59–60; 8:15; 12:5, 12; Colossians 4:12.
7. Andrew Murray, *The Ministry of Intercessory Prayer* (Minneapolis: Bethany House, 1981), 32.
8. Francis Frangipane, *In Christ's Image Training: Humility, Track Two* (Cedar Rapids, IA: Arrow Publications), 35.
9. William Zinsser, *On Writing Well* (New York: HarperPerennial, 1990), 21.
10. Alice Smith, "Praying Together: Annoying or Anointed?" *Pray!* magazine, May–June 1998, 32.
11. Public Domain, quoted in *Between Heaven and Earth* by Ken Gire (San Francisco: HarperSanFrancisco, 1997), 105.

CHAPTER TWO: THE GREAT INVITATION

1. Anonymous, *The Kneeling Christian* (Minneapolis: Zondervan, 1971), 61.
2. I highly recommend this book (*Operation World*) as a valuable intercession tool. It is now available on the Web at no cost with regular updates at http://www.gmi.org/ow.
3. See, for example, Revelation 1:8; Psalms 139:3–4; 62:11; 115:3; Proverbs 15:3; Daniel 4:35; Matthew 19:26.

CHAPTER THREE: THE CONTEMPLATIVE INTERCESSOR

1. Charles Haddon Spurgeon, *Spurgeon on Prayer and Spiritual Warfare* (New Kensington, PA: Whitaker House, 1998), 48.
2. Although Christian teaching has traditionally relegated contemplation to a mystical experience, often referred to as the soul's silent gaze toward God, I am broadening the definition here to include any spiritual discipline or practice of prayer that aids the believer in the process of growing in intimacy with Christ. For more on contemplative prayer, see my book *The Soul at Rest: A Journey into Contemplative Prayer* (Minneapolis: Bethany House, 1996).
3. Psalms 109:31; 69:33; 107:41; 113:7; 72:12–13.

CHAPTER FOUR: THE INTERCEDING LIFE

1. Wesley L. Duewel, *Mighty, Prevailing Prayer* (Grand Rapids: Zondervan, 1990), 41.
2. See http://en.wikipedia.org/wiki/ Flat_Earth_Society.
3. See *Strong's Concordance*, #5875, which translates *paracletos* as "one who pleads another's cause with one, an intercessor."
4. O. Hallesby, *Prayer* (Minneapolis: Augsburg, 1994), 78.
5. See Joy Dawson, *Forever Ruined for the Ordinary* (Nashville: Thomas Nelson, 2001) especially for practical guidance on how to hear God's voice.
6. Matthew 4:17; 6:33; 13:11, 24–52; 18:23–35; 20:1–16; 25:1–21; Acts 1:3.
7. Matthew 13:45–46; Luke 9:61–62; 18:29–30.
8. Brennan Manning, *The Signature of Jesus on the Pages of Our Lives* (Sisters, OR: Multnomah, 1992), 122.
9. For an extended, intimate journey with Jesus in His final hours, see my book *Contemplating the Cross: A Forty-Day Pilgrimage of Prayer* (Nashville: W Publishing Group, 2005).
10. Francis Frangipane, *The Power of One Christ-Like Life* (New Kensington, PA: Whitaker House, 2000), 132.
11. Rolland and Heidi Baker, *There Is Always Enough* (Kent, England: Sovereign World, 2003), 55.
12. Mother Teresa, *Works of Love Are Works of Peace: A Photographic Record* (San Francisco: Ignatius, 1996), 35.

CHAPTER FIVE: THERE'S A WAR GOING ON

1. As quoted in Duewel, *Mighty, Prevailing Prayer*, 91.
2. From a sermon by John Piper: "Be Devoted to Prayer,"

December 29, 2002. The text of this message can be found on-line at http://www.desiringgod.org/library/sermons/02/122902.html.

3. This is a direct quote from an e-mail forwarded to us by a family member of the chaplain.

4. Revelation 1:12–17.

5. Joshua 5:15; Revelation 19:11–16; Isaiah 63:3; Matthew 28:18; Revelation 4:8 NLT.

6. Revelation 5:5; Song of Solomon 2:4; Ephesians 1:20–22; 1 Corinthians 15:27.

7. C. S. Lewis, *The Screwtape Letters* (New York: Simon & Schuster, 1961), 15.

8. *Strong's Concordance*, powered by Light*Speed* Technology, © 2001–2004, StudyLight.org.

9. I am deeply indebted to Mike and Cindy Riches and Clover Creek Bible Fellowship for these truths concerning spiritual warfare that have radically impacted my life. For more on their ministry, visit www.clovercreek.org.

10. Taken from the *Online Plain Text English Dictionary*, OneLook.com.

11. Richard Foster, *Prayer: Finding the Heart's True Home* (San Francisco: HarperSanFrancisco, 1992), 249–50.

12. See 2 Corinthians 2:11; Ephesians 4:14; 6:11.

13. Watchman Nee, *Sit, Walk, Stand* (Fort Washington, PA: Christian Literature Crusade, 1972), 12–13.

CHAPTER SIX: LEARNING THE LANGUAGE OF FAITH

1. P. T. Forsyth, *The Soul of Prayer*, 5th ed. (London: Independent Press, 1966), 79.

2. See, for example, Matthew 8:9–10; 9:2, 22, 27–29; 15:28; 14:31; 17:20.

3. Hallesby, *Prayer*, 35.

4. This is a very different approach from the "word of faith" movement or the "name it, claim it" practice that has enjoyed a surge of popularity in the past decades. We do not exercise faith to get God to act, but He gives us faith and expects us to use it because He is going to act. This subtle difference is a critical one and ensures we don't slip into either legalism (it's up to us) or magic (if we follow the right steps, we can pull the answer out of the hat).

5. *Strong's Concordance*, powered by Light*Speed* Technology, © 2001–2004, StudyLight.org.

6. Donald Bloesch, *The Struggle of Prayer* (Colorado Springs: Helmers and Howard, 1988), 76.
7. The medical term for false labor pains that are a normal part of every pregnancy.
8. Duewel, *Mighty, Prevailing Prayer*, 17.

CHAPTER SEVEN: AROUND THE THRONE

1. Stephen Charnock, *The Existence and Attributes of God* (Grand Rapids: Baker, 1996), 360.
2. Though I will be referring to heaven as a "place," the reality is that God is outside of time and space, and thus a more accurate term would be "spiritual dimension."
3. Isaiah 6; Ezekiel 1:1, 26–28; see also Daniel 7; Acts 7:56.
4. Exodus 20:18–20; 34:33–35; 2 Chronicles 5:14; 7:1–3.
5. This message appears in numerous books and Internet sites under various titles. I have contacted Calvary Baptist Church in San Diego and the family members listed on their site, but was unable to obtain any further copyright information.
6. Spurgeon, *Spurgeon on Prayer and Spiritual Warfare*, 74.
7. Genesis 49:8–10; Numbers 2:1–9.
8. John Piper, *Let the Nations Be Glad* (Grand Rapids: Baker, 1993), 231.
9. For a full discourse on God's ultimate goal to gather joyful worshipers for His Son from every tribe and tongue, I would recommend the "Perspectives" course, offered in churches and schools throughout the United States through the U.S. Center for World Missions (www.perspectives.org). Also, John Piper addresses this thoroughly in the following books: *Desiring God* (pages 227–38), *The Pleasures of God* (pages 101–22), and *Let the Nations Be Glad* (chapter 1).
10. Exodus 30:7–9; 1 Chronicles 23:13; 2 Chronicles 29:11.
11. Story from United Press International, copyright 2003 by United Press International (via ClariNet), July 8, 2003, www.clari.net.
12. Michael Collopy, "Radiating Christ," taken from the Daily Prayers of the Missionaries of Charity, as presented in *Works of Love Are Works of Peace*, 202.

RESOURCES

The following books have had the greatest impact on my life in regard to a life of prayer and, in particular, intercession.

Duewel, Wesley L. *Mighty, Prevailing Prayer.* Grand Rapids: Zondervan, 1990.

Foster, Richard. *Finding the Heart's True Home.* San Francisco: HarperSanFrancisco, 1992.

Frangipane, Francis. *The Power of One Christ-Like Life.* New Kensington, PA: Whitaker House, 2000.

Hallesby, O. *Prayer.* Minneapolis: Augsburg, 1994.

Howard, Philip, and Jonathan Edwards. *The Life and Diary of David Brainerd.* Grand Rapids: Baker, 1989.

Huston, James. *A Life of Prayer: Faith and Passion for God Alone.* From the works of Teresa of Avila. Minneapolis: Bethany House, 1999.

Murray, Andrew. *The Ministry of Intercessory Prayer.* Minneapolis: Bethany House, 1981.

About the Author

TRICIA MCCARY RHODES is the author of four books on the subject of prayer and the cross, including *Contemplating the Cross*. With a B.A. in Psychology and an M.S. in Applied Social Research, Tricia spent two years as a missionary in the Alaska bush and currently travels to minister in remote areas of countries such as India and Bangladesh. In 1981 she and her husband, Joe, started New Hope Church in San Diego. She is a regular contributor to *Pray!* magazine and *Discipleship Journal* and has written articles for *Guideposts, Decision,* and *Moody Monthly.* The mother of two sons and grandmother of two, Tricia believes God's call on her life is to help others deepen their intimacy with Christ. For more information about Tricia Rhodes and her ministry, see www.soulatrest.com.

Follow this

40 DAY PILGRIMAGE OF PRAYER

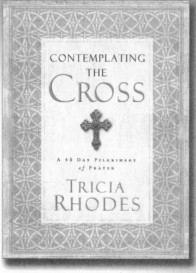

*F*ew times of year lend themselves to pilgrimage and contemplation like Easter. For forty days, Christians have before them the opportunity to examine their own path and compare it with the incredible journey undertaken by Christ, from the agony of the garden to the glory of the resurrection. By sharing her journey, Tricia Rhodes provides the tools to cultivate the cross within and the inspiration to accept the Father's summons to kneel in its shadow. Scripture and daily exercises gently nourish the spiritual traveler, while journal pages wait to hold the story of personal reflection.

More encompassing than a devotional, more intimate than a mere yardstick of faith, *Contemplating the Cross* will become a treasured keepsake for Easter and all year long.

"May God touch your deepest soul and brand you with the fire of His devotion as you contemplate the cross of Christ."
—TRICIA RHODES

W PUBLISHING GROUP
A Division of Thomas Nelson Publishers
Since 1798
www.wpublishinggroup.com